The Concept of Relevance and

the Logic Diagram Tradition

D1568698

The Concept of Relevance and

the Logic Diagram Tradition

Jan Dejnožka

Imprint: CreateSpace
Publisher: Jan Dejnožka
Ann Arbor, Michigan

Sold at Amazon.com and elsewhere

Library of Congress Cataloging Number:
2012910379

ISBN–13: 978-1475071092
ISBN–10: 1475071094

Cover photo by Jan Dejnožka

"Dejnožka challenges the reader to open his mind for a new interpretation of Russell's work, in particular that relevance notions have a greater place in his philosophy of logic than has been stressed before. Dejnožka's work is full of material which stimulates one to rethink Russell's philosophy of logic, and it is greatly to the author's credit that he brings to light such a wealth of crucial issues in the history and philosophy of logic." —Shahid Rahman

Professor Rahman teaches at the Université de Lille (France). He has served as dean and supervised many dissertations. He is the author of several books and the editor of several anthologies in logic and the philosophy of logic. He has edited a book on Hugh MacColl, written many articles and reviews, and read papers at various congresses.

"Dejnožka's erudition continues to astound me." —Nicholas Griffin

Professor Griffin is Canada Research Chair and Director of the Bertrand Russell Research Centre at McMaster University. He directs the ongoing editing of *The Collected Papers of Bertrand Russell*, now at 16 volumes. He edited *The Cambridge Companion to Bertrand Russell*, and has written several books and articles.

Table of Contents

Foreword

This book is written toward reunion in logic. I hope to reconcile modern classical logicians with relevantists through a study of the concept of relevance and its essential relationship to logic diagrams. The reconciliation on offer is that the two kinds of logic have a genus-species relationship based on their respective kinds of relevance. As an extension of this, the more general possibility of a universal logic based on relevance classifications is also explored. Of course, the reconciliation is on a purely theoretical level, but I hope it may actually help as well.

The book is based on my paper of the same name in *Logica Universalis*, vol. 4/1, pp. 67–135, 2010. The paper was an independent sequel to chapter 9 of my book, *Bertrand Russell on Modality and Logical Relevance*. Material from the paper appears by kind permission of Springer, and has been improved and expanded.

I was very happy to work with Jean-Yves Béziau, the gracious editor of *Logica Universalis*.

I thank Jon Michael Dunn, Greg Restall, Sun-Joo Shin, and Shahid Rahman for their very kind and encouraging correspondence. Once again, I thank Irving Anellis and two anonymous reviewers for their very helpful cites and corrections, and Janet Crayne, Head of Slavic and East European Division, Hatcher Graduate Library, the University of Michigan at Ann Arbor, for very kindly correcting the Bazhanov cites in the original paper. Bellucci (2019) led me to rewrite pages xiii and xv and the title of chapter 2 for greater clarity; there is no change of view.

I took the cover photo in Niskayuna, New York. The original photo is date stamped February 1981.

Wake Forest, North Carolina
October 10, 2019

Introduction

What is logical relevance? Alan Ross Anderson and Nuel D. Belnap say in their first volume of *Entailment* that the "modern classical tradition[,] stemming from Frege and Whitehead-Russell, gave no consideration whatsoever to the classical notion of relevance," which was "central to logic from the time of Aristotle" (Anderson 1975: xxi; see 17). But just what is this classical notion? I shall argue in this book that Anderson and Belnap misunderstand the relevance tradition on the sense in which a valid argument's premisses contain its conclusion.[1] For the relevance tradition is implicitly most deeply concerned with the containment of truth-grounds, less deeply with the containment of classes, and least of all with variable sharing in the Anderson-Belnap manner. Thus modern classical logicians such as Peirce, Frege, Russell, Wittgenstein, and Quine are implicit relevantists on the deepest level.

To show this, I shall reunite two fields of logic which, strangely from the traditional point of view, have become basically separated from each other: relevance logic and diagram logic. They are reunited in my main argument as follows: 1. If the premisses of an argument contain its conclusion, then the argument is relevantly valid. 2. If at least one diagram of the premisses of an argument also diagrams its conclusion, then the premisses contain the conclusion. 3. Modus ponens, disjunctive syllogism, and many other arguments that violate Anderson-Belnap variable sharing can be and have been so diagrammed. 4. Therefore such arguments are relevantly valid. Relevantists accept premiss (1) but reject conclusion (4). They overlook premisses (2) and (3), which belong to the other field, diagram logic.[2] I see no equivocation on "contain" in premisses (1) and (2). In fact, it is hard to think of anything more relevant to showing relevant containment than diagramming it. What else could the relevance tradition have had in mind, with its whole-part containment theory of deductive inference and its thousands of diagrams of logical inference?

I am rejecting only the relevantists' rejection of modern classical logic as irrelevantist. I am by no means rejecting their positive views on relevance, which I see as a complementary study of a very different *secondary* branch of the logical and historical tree of relevance. The branches overlap, with the truth-ground containment branch underlying what may be very broadly called the intensional branch. The general principle is that what is intensionally (or relevantistically) relevant is also extensionally (or classically) relevant; but the converse does not hold. At least this is so insofar as relevantists merely require a stronger, more restrictive kind of valid inference than modern classical logicians do, and would not regard as valid any inference the latter regard as invalid, that is, would not regard as valid any inference where the conclusion logically can be false even if all the premisses are true, per modern classical truth table.

As I see it, the irony is that precisely because the great modern classical logicians Peirce, Frege, Russell, Wittgenstein, and Quine made the concept of truth-ground relevance so pure and transparent, and so clearly different from that of intensional relevance, which in effect they banished from their own logics as unneeded for purposes of truth preservation, that some recent logicians failed to see that the primary concept of relevance was kept, and concluded that relevance had been abandoned altogether. These logicians then went off to recover intensional relevance, which, though it is not at all a *wrong* track, is a secondary (or at least not the only) track. The result was a sort of mutual excommunication.

In chapters (1)–(4), I discuss premisses (1)–(3) and conclusion (4) of my main argument in order. In (5), I discuss the argument's significance in terms of two broad conceptions of relevance. In (6), I reply to objections and state my view. In (7), I summarize definitions, theses, and constraints for modern classical relevance. In (8), I offer my conclusions, and briefly explore the more general possibility of a universal logic based on relevance classifications.

I shall examine mainly propositional logic, and mainly modus ponens (ponendum) and disjunctive syllogism (modus tollendum ponens). Modern classical logic admits them as valid. Anderson and Belnap not only reject them, but consider their rejection the litmus test of relevance. Richard Sylvan makes this definitional: "In brief, *relevant* logics are those sociative logics which reject Disjunctive Syllogism...and associated forms" (Sylvan 2000: 12).[3] But my argument also applies to modern classical quantificational logic, which can be and has been diagrammed as well. That has been done in at least three ways: Vennis balls, truth tables, and rewriting (diagrams of) propositional logic as (diagrams of) quantificational logic.

Diagrams of invalid arguments cannot show conclusion containment. Diagrams of valid arguments fall into two classes: those that visibly show conclusion containment, and those that do not. Venn's do, and Frege's do not. (Venn's are designed to, and Frege's are not.) Those that do not can still be used to prove validity using rules of inference, tree methods, truth tables, or the like.

It is the essence of visibly valid logic diagrams to apply the concept of relevance. It is what they do. To show containment of the conclusion is to show its entailment. And if we find one diagram that does that, we need not look for more.

If it is unclear what a diagram is, we may speak more deeply and generally of logic notations. We may say that if, in at least one notation of an argument, we notate the conclusion in the very act of notating the premisses, then the premisses contain the conclusion. We may then rewrite the title of this book as, *The Concept of Relevance and the Logic Notation Tradition.*

1. Containment of the Conclusion
Shows Logical Relevance

We begin with premiss (1) of my main argument, which I take to be non-controversial. It merely states the ordinary intuitive core notion of relevance from which everyone must begin.

Relevantists try to make formally precise certain initial intuitive formulations of what relevance is, such as that a relevant conclusion is "related to," "connected to," or "follows from" the premisses (Anderson 1975: 17).[1] But the key conception they try to make precise is "containment" of the conclusion in the premisses (Anderson 1975: 155). The ancient insight behind this is that it is (a) impossible for the conclusion to be false if all the premisses are true if and only if (b) the conclusion does not, in some appropriate sense, go beyond what the premisses assert (Sextus Empiricus 1933: ch. 17). If such containment is made precise, then the antecedent of this biconditional will become clear as well, since the consequent will explain it. This means specifying formal conditions for a logic that satisfy the intension of "relevant containment," so that its syntax and its extensional semantics (domain and/or truth-conditions) determine containment relevance. That is, "[formal deductive] logic is a *formal* matter, and...validity...depends...on formal considerations alone" (Anderson 1975: 14, their emphasis). I agree. We should be trying to capture the intension of "contain" extensionally as best we can. I merely note that this is at bottom just the sort of containment which logicians have been diagramming for centuries. Of course, the logic diagram tradition is not the entire logical relevance tradition, which is quite variegated (most logicians use verbal logics, and logicians generally have not diagrammed relevance *fallacies*), much less the whole Western logic tradition, which is by no means unanimous on accepting modus ponens or disjunctive syllogism. I merely hold that the relevantists overlook the best and, so to speak, most visible concept of their own tradition: diagram containment. But appearances can be deceiving here. Much depends on what a diagram is. Much also depends on what containment is, and on what it is containment of. What, then, is containment?

Anderson and Belnap admit containment as the core intuitive notion of logical relevance. They approve of the traditional theory that the conclusion of a logically relevant argument is always in some sense contained in the premises (Anderson 1975: 155). For them the only issue is how to make this notion technically clear.

Anderson and Belnap give this series of definitions:

> We shall say that a primitive entailment $A \rightarrow B$ is *explicitly tautological* if some (conjoined) atom of A is identical with some (disjoined) atom of B. Such entailments may be thought of as satisfying the classical dogma that for A to entail B, B must be "contained" in A. (Anderson 1975: 155)

They give no rationale for this definition at all. They simply say, "We...think it obvious" that their requirement for primitive entailment is correct (Anderson 1975: 154). There is no doubt that any inference that meets the test is valid, since the test boils down to using simplification, $(P \& Q) \rightarrow P$, to arrive at the conjoined atom of the premiss, then addition (also called disjunction), $P \rightarrow (P \lor Q)$, to arrive at the conclusion via the disjoined atom. Simplification and addition are on the initial list of "good guys" (Anderson 1975: 154). Granted, some writers consider addition to be paradoxical, at least in some contexts (see Weingartner 1994: 93 on Hesse's confirmation paradox, 97 on Ross's deontic paradox); but I suspect these special contexts involve problems of paraphrase which do not affect propositional logic as such. Possibly this choice of beginnings is result-driven. In any case, the question for us is whether the Anderson-Belnap definition, which limits primitive entailment to whatever passes this limited simplification-addition test, *excludes* any good guys. (Note that it would be circular to use the test to justify simplification and addition, since they basically constitute the test.) Anderson and Belnap generalize their definition so as to handle more complex arguments as follows:

> We...call an entailment $A_1 \vee ... \vee A_m \rightarrow B_1 \&... \& B_n$ in normal form *explicitly tautological* (extending the previous definition) iff for every A_i and B_j, $A_i \rightarrow B_j$ is explicitly tautological (sharing); and we take such entailments to be valid iff explicitly tautological. (Anderson 1975: 156)

Then they sum up:

> We call an entailment $A \rightarrow B$ where A and B are purely truth functional, a *tautological entailment*, if $A \rightarrow B$ has a normal form $A_1 \vee ... \vee A_m \rightarrow B_1 \&... \& B_n$ which is explicitly tautological. (Anderson 1975: 157)

I take this to mean that tautological entailment has two conditions: (1) the inference is tautological in the sense of modern classical validity, i.e., truth preservation; and (2) this variable sharing requirement: where an atom is an atomic statement or its negation, there must be *some* way to rewrite the conjoined premisses in disjunctive normal form (a disjunction of conjunctions of atoms), and *some* way to rewrite the conclusion in conjunctive normal form (a conjunction of disjunctions of atoms), so that *each* disjunct of the premisses' normal form contains *some* conjoined atom that is identical with *some* disjoined atom in *each* conjunct of the conclusion's normal form. This may be called their *atomic (or variable sharing) requirement*. The disjunctive normal form for the premisses is basically a way to represent the truth table, with each disjunct of A representing a row on which all the premisses are true.

This atomic requirement prevents hypothetical syllogism from being a tautological entailment:

> As an example, we show that $(p \supset q)$ & $(q \supset r) \rightarrow p \supset r$ is invalid. By the definition of "$\supset$," we have $(\neg p \lor q)$ & $(\neg q \lor r) \rightarrow \neg p \lor r$ which has a normal form, $(\neg p$ & $\neg q) \lor (\neg p$ & $r) \lor (q$ & $\neg q) \lor (q$ & $r) \rightarrow \neg p \lor r$. But q & $\neg q \rightarrow \neg p \lor r$ is not an explicitly tautological entailment; hence the candidate fails. (Anderson 1975: 157, my negation sign)

They argue that in their own logic, "if $A \rightarrow B$ and $B \rightarrow C$ are tautological entailments, so also is $A \rightarrow C$" (Anderson 1975: 160). But their dismissal of modern classical hypothetical syllogism will make Aristotelian syllogistic a chief stumbling block for them later on.

The atomic requirement also kills disjunctive syllogism (Anderson 1975: 165). Or as they would more simply say, disjunctive syllogism is the inference of Q from $(P \lor Q)$ and $\neg P$, where Q is any old statement and need not have any intensional relationship to P. It also kills modus ponens. Or as they would more simply say, modus ponens is the inference of Q from $(P \supset Q)$ and P, where Q is any old statement and need not have any intensional relationship to P. The proof is simple in each case. The modus ponens premisses go from P & $(P \supset Q)$ to the logically equivalent P & $(\neg P \lor Q)$, then to normal form $(P$ & $\neg P) \lor (P$ & $Q)$ using distribution, one of the rules Anderson and Belnap allow for converting the conjoined premisses to disjunctive normal form (Anderson 1975: 156). Clearly the first disjunct, $(P \,\&\, \neg P)$, fails to contain the sole atom of the conclusion, Q. Disjunctive syllogism is even easier. The conjunction of its premisses goes directly into the very same normal form by distribution, with the same result.

It seems better to say that Anderson and Belnap are really objecting to the treatment of these argument forms as relevant argument forms. That is, following Robert K. Meyer on modus ponens (1985: 584), it seems better to say the argument forms really at issue here are not $(P \,\&\, (P \supset Q)) \supset Q$ (modern classical modus ponens) or $((P \lor Q) \,\&\, \neg P) \supset Q$ (modern classical disjunctive syllogism), but $(P \,\&\, (P \supset Q)) \rightarrow Q$ (relevant modus ponens) and $((P \lor Q) \,\&\, \neg P) \rightarrow Q$ (relevant disjunctive syllogism). (Here I have given the conditionals that correspond to the argument forms.) Similarly for modern classical hypothetical syllogism and relevant hypothetical syllogism. For Anderson and Belnap are not denying that the modern classical forms satisfy condition (1), modern classical validity. They are only denying that they satisfy condition (2), Anderson-Belnap variable sharing. If so, then the question is how to interpret "$\rightarrow$" ("entails"). Of course, "$\supset$" ("materially implies") is defined by its truth table as meaning "false if the antecedent is true and the consequent false, and otherwise true." I will be arguing in effect that the very diagrams that show the mentioned three modern classical argument forms to be truth-ground containment relevant also show the three mentioned relevant argument forms to be valid in virtue of that very fact. That is, I will be arguing that extensional truth-ground relevance may be defined as follows: $P \rightarrow Q$ =Df the truth-grounds of P contain the truth-grounds of Q. And I shall be arguing that this is the most basic kind of logical relevance.

There are two main ways to defend modern classical logic from all this criticism. First, we may deny that relevance is a necessary condition of deductive validity, and affirm that it is a sufficient condition of deductive validity *simply* that it is impossible for the conclusion to be false if the premisses are true. At least two relevantists have claimed that this is literally all there is to the modern classical view (Read 1988: 19–20; Mares 2004: 3–4). On this approach, we would be agreeing with Read and Mares that modern classical logic is not relevance logic, but we would be disagreeing with their view that this means it is bad logic. Apparently Anderson and Belnap think this is the line Bertrand Russell, whom they regard as their chief nemesis, would take. Or second, we may hold that there is more to modern classical logic than mere validity; namely, modern classical logic is relevant after all, even if that does not accord with the relevantists' conception of what relevance is. This is the approach we shall take here, as a matter of both logic and scholarship.

2. Visibly Valid Diagrams Show the Premisses Contain the Conclusion

We come to premiss (2) of my main argument. What is the traditional test of entailment? Is it the variable sharing requirement of Anderson and Belnap? No, that is their new invention. Traditionally, it is the diagram test. What is a logic diagram? Martin Gardner says, "A logic diagram is a two-dimensional geometric figure with spatial relations that are isomorphic with the structure of a logical statement" (Gardner 1968: 28). Gardner infers that a diagram and a statement "are simply two ways of asserting the same thing....It would be foolish to ask which of the two, considered in itself, is superior to the other" (Gardner 1968: 28). We can choose any diagram we please, and we can choose any features of the diagram we please to represent any logical parts of a statement we please, so long as the representation is isomorphic. But if I may improve on Gardner, diagrams can be multi-dimensional. And a *successful* diagram is one in which a valid conclusion is diagrammed in the very act of diagramming the premisses. For our purposes here, I think this much will suffice, even though there are many issues on what a diagram is; see Shimojima (2001: 5–27), Stenning (2001: 32), and Cheng (2001: 84–85). Premiss (2) says nothing about what logic diagrams represent in the sense of offering a theory of what they are about, for example, a theory of propositional content. It merely says that showing containment by a diagram is a *sufficient condition* of relevant containment. For our purposes, that need not even be a necessary condition of relevant containment. As far as I know, every known form of relevantist inference can be diagrammed. (Every known form of valid modern classical inference can be, and that is a wider class.) But at least in theory, it is always possible that just around the corner, there is some exotic new form of relevant inference that cannot be diagrammed.[1] We need not deny this in order for our argument that modern classical logic is relevant to succeed. But it may still be of interest to ask what logic diagrams represent.

Visibly valid diagrams represent logical containments. But what are the containments *of*? Surely not of linguistic expressions, since language may vary while content remains the same. But we do not want the containments to be of propositional contents if we can help it, since the notion of a proposition is controversial. One theory, basically due to Leonhard Euler, is that the diagrams' "spatial inclusions and exclusions correspond to the nonspatial inclusions and exclusions of classes" (Copi 1978: 197–98; see Edwards 2004: 12). The containments are of members or of sub-classes by classes; class intersections and exclusions are also represented. This answer is correct as far as it goes, and is already extensional semantics (Greaves 2002: 121–37). But Wittgenstein gives a more general answer which is not limited to class containments. Namely, logic diagrams represent the containment of truth-possibilities, specifically, of truth-grounds. Wittgenstein says in the *Tractatus* (1969/1921):

> T 5.101....I will give the name *truth-grounds* of a proposition to those **truth-possibilities** of its truth-arguments that make it true.
>
> T 5.11 If all the truth-grounds that are common to a number of propositions are at the same time truth-grounds of a certain proposition, then we say that the truth of that proposition **follows from** the truth of the others.
>
> T 5.12 In particular, the truth of a proposition '*p*' **follows from** the truth of another proposition '*q*' if all the truth-grounds of the latter are truth-grounds of the former.
>
> T 5.121 The truth-grounds of the one are **contained in** those of the

other: *p* **follows from** *q*.

T 5.122 If *p* **follows from** *q*, the sense of '*p*' is **contained in** the sense of '*q*'.

T 5.132 If *p* **follows from** *q*, I can make an inference from *q* to *p*, deduce *p* from *q*. (Wittgenstein's italic emphasis, my bold emphasis)

T 5.11, 5.12, and 5.122 say that if *q*'s truth-grounds contain those of *p*, then *p* follows from *q*. That is, *p* follows from *q* if, on all possible combinations of truth-possibilities, whenever *q* is true, *p* is true. T 5.122 says the same for the sense of "*p*" and "*q*"; the sense is like an instruction for figuring out the truth-value of a statement from its truth-grounds. Thus *q*'s truth-ground containment of *p* and *p*'s following from *q* are logically equivalent for Wittgenstein. This implies in turn that truth-ground containment and following from contain and follow from each other, whether or not "contain" and "follow from" are the same in sense. (T 5.122 appears to imply that they contain each other's sense.)

Surely Wittgenstein's thesis, that for a conclusion to follow, i.e., for it to be relevantly valid, is for its truth-grounds to be contained in the truth-grounds of the premisses, is implicit in the relevance tradition, and is what logicians most deeply had in mind, or ought to have had in mind, all along. Surely truth-ground containment is also what logicians have most deeply been diagramming all along, implicitly if not always with full awareness. If this is correct, we may say that the truth has been hiding in plain sight from the relevantists for a long time.

Wittgenstein does not use the terms "relevant" or "entailment." But he expressly equates truth-ground containment with following from, which is what relevant entailment *is*. Thus it seems that Wittgenstein is not only a relevantist, but crowns the relevance tradition by expressly stating the deepest and most illuminating theory of what is contained in logical containment, namely, truth-grounds. And if he is right, then the two possible ways I described of defending Russell against Anderson and Belnap coalesce. For truth preservation, or modern classical validity, is precisely containment of truth-grounds, or Wittgensteinian relevance.[2]

Wittgenstein's theory is the best one for explaining the sense in which Russell is a relevantist, since Russell expressly endorses the theory, as we shall see shortly.

In connection with truth-ground containment, we may offer a theory of propositional contents of our own if we wish.[3] Or we may apply Wittgenstein's theory or Russell's theory of propositional contents. Or we may advocate no theory of propositional content at all, and simply use truth-grounds.

On Wittgenstein's picture theory of meaning, *every* proposition is a "logical picture" that has "pictorial form" in "logical space." "Propositions *show* the logical form of reality. They display it" (T 4.121). These pictures sound like diagrams.

Russell's theory of propositions of the same time period is arguably very similar (McDonough 1986: 145–158). Russell's logic is diagrammatic in the sense that it is meant to be an ideal language mirroring the structure of the world. Russell says, "[I]n a logically correct symbolism there will always be a certain fundamental identity of structure between a fact and the symbol for it;...the complexity of the symbol corresponds very closely with the complexity of the facts symbolized by it" (Russell 1971/1918: 197). He says that the language of *Principia Mathematica* was intended to be "completely analytic [in that it] will show at a glance the logical structure of the facts asserted or denied" (Russell 1971/1918: 198). But we need not enter the murky waters of Russell-Wittgenstein comparisons on ideal language theory here. All we need to show Russell's relevantism is his express endorsement of Wittgenstein's view that logical deducibility is always a matter of containment of truth-grounds.[4]

Both Russell and Wittgenstein expressly tie the concept of containment to the concept of following from. But it might seem that they are merely endorsing the "ideology" (intension) of relevance without providing an "ontology" (extension), i.e., without specifying just how their logics consist of relevant containments.[5] That is, despite their relevantist *talk*, it might seem that their logics might actually *be* irrelevantist. And this, of course, is just what relevantists actually believe.

Lets us see, then, if the logics of Russell and of Wittgenstein can be diagrammed to show containment of the conclusion in the premisses. Now, they themselves rarely, if ever, provide literally geometrical diagrams in the manner of Euler, Venn, or Peirce. Wittgenstein does use an "intuitive method" of brackets and lines to show tautology (T 6.1203). But for the most part it is others who provide literally geometrical diagrams for modern classical logic. This brings us to premiss (3) of my main argument.

3. Modern Classical Logic Can Be
Diagrammed to Show Containment

Whether propositional logic has been or can be diagrammed depends in part on what diagrams are. I hold that it can be and has been diagrammed in at least three main ways: truth tables, truth trees, and literally geometrical figures such as circles or squares. I shall discuss each way in turn.

First, truth tables are logic diagrams as defined by Gardner. Their two-dimensional spatial features are rows and columns of truth-values. We can make a truth table literally geometrical by representing the truth-values as spatial points, i.e., as the intersections of vertical and horizontal lines, with "T" and "F" as names of the points. Or we can take out the letters and use different sorts of dots at the intersections to represent the points. Or we can draw a square around each truth-value so as to result in a rectangular diagram. We can then take out the letters and use different shadings within the squares to represent truth and falsehood. Or if shading is not geometrical as such, we can use squares for truth and circles for falsehood, so as to result in rows and columns of squares and circles.

Even if the truth tables we customarily draw are not literally geometrical diagrams, since they consist of rows and columns of letters instead of lines or figures, they are still diagrams in the broad sense of being spatial representations of the logical structures of the premisses and conclusion. Of course this is moot, since we can also use line intersections or geometrical figures to represent truth-values. In fact, the whole question of geometricality is moot. The only thing that is relevant is that in the very act of representing the truth-grounds of the premisses, we already represent the truth-grounds of the conclusion. It does not matter whether truth tables are literally, purely, or totally geometrical, or even geometrical at all. Visible containment is the key, not geometricality as such. And in all of the diagrams just discussed, containment of the conclusion is shown when every combination of truth-possibilities of the constituent atomic statements on which all the premisses are true is also a combination on which the conclusion is true. Thus we can keep our "T" and "F," or even write "True" and "False."

Of course, modus ponens and disjunctive syllogism are shown valid by their truth tables in the propositional calculus. We also know that truth tables visually depict containments of truth-grounds. What has been missing is only the awareness of what this means for modern classical logic as relevant. Indeed, when Russell endorses Wittgenstein's view that truth tables show containment of truth-grounds, we see that both of them are express relevantists. For the equation of containment with following from is expressly stated in the texts. The only thing missing is the mere label "relevant" or "entailment" which we would use today.

And what are truth trees, if not diagrams that represent the flow of containment of truth-grounds? Diagramming the containment of truth-grounds is what truth trees are all about. They show that containment of truth-grounds can be diagrammed as truth-flow along the branches of a tree, where the branches can be drawn as statements connected by sequences of geometrical line segments. Thus, insofar as truth-ground containment is relevant containment, truth trees show that modern classical logic is just as relevant as is relevantist logic.

Jeffrey's (1967) trees are not purely geometrical, since his line segments are broken up by linguistic statements at the nodes. But this is moot for two reasons. First, we can just as easily draw the segments as continuous geometrical branchings with the statements to the side of each intersection. Second and more deeply, the whole issue of literal geometricality is moot. What counts is whether the trees show containment of truth-grounds.

Perhaps the chief objection to Jeffrey's trees is that they do not support my main argument unless the complete diagramming of the tree counts as the complete diagramming of the premisses. For otherwise a valid conclusion is not diagrammed in the very act of diagramming the premisses, but is discovered to be valid later, even if by a finite and wholly mechanical process. If so, then my main argument cannot rely on trees, but only on truth tables and literally geometrical diagrams. But I would say the whole tree is the whole diagram. Even a Venn diagram must be drawn in a series of temporal steps, or at least over time. At least this is true of anything drawn by hand.

Of course, in Jeffrey trees, we diagram only that there is *no* possible combination of atomic truth-values on which all the premisses are true and the conclusion *false*. But that is to show by contraposition that the truth-grounds of the conclusion are contained in the truth-grounds of the premisses. Such trees are better called negative or falsifiability trees, as opposed to truth trees proper, which flow in a forward direction to prove a positive conclusion (Anellis 1990a).

Third, literally geometrical diagrams may seem merely analogical in comparison to tables and trees, which seem to show truth-ground containment more literally. Tables and trees show that truth-grounds, not classes, are what is most deeply contained in logical inference. But we need to understand the whole tradition if we are to understand modern classical logic's place in it.

Aristotle seems primarily concerned with attribute intensions in his syllogistic (Greaves 2002: chs. 8–9). But even Aristotle apparently uses literally geometrical diagrams that can be interpreted in extensional terms (Greaves 2002: 116–17), yielding a logically equivalent extensional syllogistic (compare Greaves 2002: 130–31). Then the Stoics implicitly use truth tables. Then Euler uses literally geometrical diagrams expressly to show class inclusions (Greaves 2002: ch. 9). Then Kant diagrams disjunctive syllogism. Then Bolzano defines deducibility as the relation that all ideas which make the premises true, when substituted for the variable parts in them, also make the conclusion true when substituted for the same variable parts in it (Bolzano 1972/1837: § 155.2). Bolzano says it is "customary" to call this *following from*, and says it "has great similarity to the relation between including and included ideas" (Bolzano 1972/1837: § 155.2). Venn improves logic diagrams, and Peirce diagrams both propositional and quantificational logic. Boole and Frege use truth tables implicitly (on Frege, see Bynum 1972: 14, 14n.17; Heijenoort 1967a: 2), and Peirce, Müller, Russell, Wittgenstein, and Post use them expressly. Then Wittgenstein expressly states that truth tables show that *following from* equates to containment of truth-grounds. Then Russell endorses this. Then Quine uses *both* truth tables and Venn diagrams. Then a group of tableau and tree logicians develops truth trees to show the logical flow of truth-ground containment. Then it is discovered that Lewis Carroll had used trees for syllogistic. Then the relevantists astonishingly announce in effect that all this is both untraditional and a big mistake, and that none of it has anything to do with relevance or with containment of the conclusion in the premises.

There are two main ways to validate propositional logic using literally geometrical diagrams. First, we can rewrite propositional logic as quantificational logic and diagram the rewritten statements. In effect, we would be treating truth-ground containments as class inclusions. (Of course, class-containments *are* a kind of truth-conditions.) Or second, we can try to diagram propositional logic directly. I shall discuss these two approaches in order.

The first approach is simply to replace singular statements with logically equivalent universal statements. For example, "Socrates runs," or Rs, is rewritable as $(x)((x = s) \supset Rx)$, or "If anything is identical to Socrates, then it runs." We can add $(\exists x)(x = s)$ for existential import if we wish, and we can rewrite statements with multiple singular logical subject-terms in much the same way. This approach has traditional antecedents. Arnauld (1964/1683: 207) treats singular judgments as universal. "In *De Arte Combinatoria* (1666), Leibniz already held that singulars are to be regarded as universal propositions" (Grimm 1993: 312). Russell's student Irving Copi quotes Kant: "'Logicians are justified in saying that, in the employment of judgments in syllogisms, singular judgments can be treated like those that are universal'" (Copi 1978: 229, citing Kant 1965/1787: A71/B96; see 1988/1800: 107). Kant continues, "For, since they have no extension at all, the predicate cannot relate to part only of that which is contained in the concept of the subject, and be excluded from the rest" (Kant 1965/1787: A71/B96; see 1988/1800: 107–8). John Stuart Mill says that there are no special syllogistic forms for singular propositions "because, their predicate being affirmed or denied of the whole of the subject, they are ranked, for the purposes of the syllogism, with universal propositions" (Mill 2002/1891: 109; see 109n.) Lewis Carroll says, "A Proposition, whose Subject is an *Individual*, is to be regarded as *Universal*" (Carroll 1977/1896: 68; see 69; 1958/1887: 57). Carroll says,

> Now what would you make of such a Proposition as "The Cake you have given me is nice"? Is it Particular, or Universal? "Particular, of course," you readily reply. "One single Cake is hardly worth calling 'some', even." No, my dear impulsive Reader, it is 'Universal'. Remember that, few as they are (and I grant you they couldn't well be fewer), they are (or rather 'it is') *all* that you have given me! (Carroll 1958/1887: 10)

Stated more traditionally, quantity in an Aristotelian categorical statement is determined by whether the extension of the subject-term is covered to the "widest or fullest extent," in which case the quantity is universal ("all"), or whether "only part of the subject" is covered, in which case it is particular ("some") (Creighton 1898: 81). "But since it is impossible to limit a singular subject, individual propositions are to be regarded as universal. They belong, that is, to the class of propositions which employ the subject term in its complete extent" (Creighton 1898: 81). (Kant denies that singular terms *have* extensions, but by that very fact agrees that they lack *limitable* or *partitionable* extensions. No doubt he deems extensions necessarily possibly plural, so that not only singular terms but also Fregean sortal terms such as "even prime number" are extensionless.) In medieval times, "Lambert of Auxerre (or Lagny) [used the] formulation 'Everything that is Socrates runs, Socrates is a man, therefore a man runs'" (Ashworth 2006). But not all medieval logicians rewrote singular statements as universal statements (Ashworth 2006). And some logicians have recently argued that singular subjects "can be taken as having either particular or universal quantity" (Englebretsen 1998: 73). But I will rewrite singular statements as universal statements here.[1]

Copi adapts Venn diagrams so as to diagram arguments in modern classical quantificational logic (Copi 1978: 205–13). Copi adds that any old singular proposition "S is P" can be rewritten as "All objects in unit class S are in predicate class P" (Copi 1978: 228–29). Modus ponens emerges as one of the two valid forms of mixed hypothetical syllogism (Copi 1978: 251). And if we have modus ponens, then we also have disjunctive syllogism, since they are equivalent.

Or we can rewrite modus ponens using "All P-situations are Q-situations" for "If P, then Q," and "All (actual) true-situations are P-situations" for "P is true," or more simply "P." Then modus ponens becomes a syllogism whose conclusion is "All true-situations are Q-situations," representing "Q is true," or more simply "Q." This is categorical syllogism Barbara, mood and figure AAA–1, which is shown valid by Venn diagram. We can rewrite disjunctive syllogism by first rewriting premiss "P or Q" as its equivalent, "If not P, then Q," then rewriting that equivalent quantificationally as "All Not-P-situations are Q-situations." Then we rewrite premiss "Not-P" as "All true-situations are Not-P-situations." Thus we first rewrite disjunctive syllogism as modus ponens, and then rewrite modus ponens as Barbara, much as before. Once again the conclusion is "All true-situations are Q-situations," which rewrites back to "Q." "True-situations," of course, equates to "truth-grounds," and "Q-situations" to "Q-grounds."

We can also rewrite "P is true" as "There are no cases in the Universe in which P is false" (see Bocheński 1961: 309). Thus "propositional logic is made to appear as a discipline co-ordinate with, if not subordinate to, the logic of classes" (Bocheński 1961: 309).[2] And this raises a deeper issue. Namely, granting the mutual rewritability of propositional and quantificational logic (Gardner 1968: 49), which logic, if either, is logically basic? Englebretsen has a good discussion of this (Englebretsen 1998: 67–75), but for our purposes it does not matter. I merely note that this mutual rewritability ought to end Quine's reluctance to extend truth tables to quantification because they would be infinitely large (Quine 1983: 55). For we can simply rewrite quantificational logic as propositional logic first.

But suppose we do not wish to rewrite propositional logic as quantificational logic. Suppose we think that is not strictly correct, or is even contrived and artificial, and to that extent a distortion. Can propositional logic be diagrammed directly? Gardner says:

> The propositional calculus first arose...as an interpretation of the class calculus. The correspondence between the two calculi is so close that every class statement has a corresponding propositional form. For example, "All *A* is *B*" can be interpreted to mean, "If *X* is a member of class *A*, then *X* is a member of class *B*." Similarly, "If *A* is true than *B* is true" may be interpreted to mean, "The class of all occasions on which *A* is true is

included in the class of occasions on which *B* is true....Every statement in truth-functional logic has a similar class analogue. As the diagramming of these statements makes clear, they are simply different verbal ways of stating the same underlying logical structure.

> To use the Venn circles for propositional logic we must first interpret them in a different way. Each circle now stands for a proposition which may be either true or false, rather than a class which may or may not have members. (Gardner 1968: 49)

Gardner then diagrams material implication, saying enough to show how to diagram modus ponens, and a fortiori, disjunctive syllogism (Gardner 1968: 50).

Venn diagrams which directly represent propositional logic are in effect just truth tables using intersecting circles instead of intersecting lines (truth trees) or intersecting rows and columns of squares (truth tables). And just like row and column truth tables, Venn diagrams can handle any finite number of terms, if we draw them in three dimensions (Edwards 2004). Thus "Vennis balls," as Edwards calls them, and truth tables are always mutually rewritable for any finite number of terms.

Kant describes two ways to diagram disjunctive syllogism directly. First:

> The logical determination of a concept by reason is based upon a disjunctive syllogism, in which the major premiss contains a logical division (the division of the sphere of a universal concept), the minor premiss limiting this sphere to a certain part, and the conclusion determining the concept by means of this part. (Kant 1965/1787: A576–77/B604–5; compare Kant 1988/1800: 107 on spheres of judgments)

Second, Venn says, "Kant (*Logik* I. § 29) [is] one of the very few logicians who have given a diagram to illustrate disjunctives" (Venn 1971/1894: 524). Venn says Kant "take[s] a square and divide[s] it up into four smaller squares; these...make up between them the whole sphere of the divided concept" (Venn 1971/1894: 524); see Kant's diagram and discussion (Kant 1988/1800: 113–14). Kant, like Johann Heinrich Lambert and many others, considers only exclusive disjunction (Venn 1971/1894: 524), since it suits "the subordination of a [mutually exclusive and jointly exhaustive] plurality of species to a genus" in classificatory science (Venn 1971/1894: 522). Venn diagrams both inclusive and exclusive disjunction, using overlapping circles and shadings (Venn 1971/1894: 124–25).

Since geometry is synthetic and logic is analytic for Kant, is a geometrical representation of a logical argument a problem for him? Different answers might be suggested. (1) It might be a problem for him, but not for us. (2) It is only a representation. (1) and (2) are bad answers. The representation is supposed to be perspicuous. The best answer is (3) Whole-part containments are analytic for Kant. Kant says in the *Critique of Pure Reason*, "Some few fundamental propositions, presupposed by the geometrician, are, indeed, really analytic, and rest on the principle of contradiction....; for instance,... the whole is equal to itself; or... the whole is greater than its part" (Kant 1965/1787: B16–17). He repeats the point in the *Prolegomena* (Kant 1950 / 1783: 17). This clearly implies that whole-part containments in literally geometrical diagrams of valid logic arguments represent analytic inferences for Kant. Thus not only does Kant diagram disjunctive syllogism to show containment of the conclusion in the premises, but it seems evident that he would take the diagram to rest on a fundamental principle *presupposed* by geometry that he considers to be analytic. And as he accepts disjunctive syllogism in his formal linguistic logic, he obviously does find it analytic. In fact, Anderson and Belnap's citation of Kant as their traditional authority on "The principle of 'containment'" as ground of "analytic truth" (Anderson 1975: 155) appears badly misplaced and ironic in their whole critique of modern classical logic.[3]

Quine diagrams what is virtually disjunctive syllogism by Venn diagram. Quine says:

> Actually, the diagrams can be used somewhat more widely; e.g., in
> arguing from the
> Premisses: Everyone east of the tracks is either slovenly or poor,
>   Not everyone east of the tracks is poor
> to the
> Conclusion: Some slovenly persons are not poor.
> We set up a three circle diagram as usual...(Quine 1959: 79)

Peirce diagrams the whole of propositional logic directly. Peirce designed his graphs to "make both the logical structure and the entailments of propositions directly observable" (Greaves 2002: 172). "Peirce's goal [was] that a notation also be designed to turn the process of proof into an observational science" (Greaves 2002: 178). Methods for translating Peirce's graphs into propositional logic, showing consistency and weak completeness, have been available for decades (Hammer 1996: 130 citing Roberts 1973 and Zeman 1964; see also White 1984). If we specify syntax ("wfd" means well-formed diagram), semantics, axioms, and rules of proof, we can construct neo-Peircean formal diagram propositional logics for which we can prove soundness and completeness. Roberts and Sowa do this for Peirce's propositional graph logic indirectly by rewriting propositional graph logic as propositional linguistic logic and showing equivalence. (This must not be confused with rewriting propositional logic as quantificational logic.) Each does this somewhat differently. See Roberts (1973: 132, Appendix 2, Table of Logical

Notations; see 45, 139 on modus ponens.) But Shin does this for a Venn-style propositional diagram logic directly, that is, without first translating it into propositional linguistic logic, quantificational logic, or anything else (Shin 1994: ch. 3; see 2002: ch. 4). Stenning and Lemon miss the whole point of Shin's book when they say, "The essential idea here, then, is to 'translate' diagrammatic representations into logical representations" (Stenning 2001: 38).

Shin shows that the soundness and completeness proofs for her diagram logic are logically independent of the soundness and completeness proofs for the corresponding linguistic logic, though she admits the proofs are similar due to the general nature of propositional logic. This is a fine achievement, but even Shin recognizes only part of it. She knows she has vindicated literally geometrical diagram logic as being formally as precise as linguistic logic. But she does not realize what this means for the concept of relevance, or for the relevance of modern classical logic.

Kuzičév (1968) gives "a correspondence between Venn diagrams and formulas of propositional calculus" (Ferebee 1975: 70).

Wright gives square diagrams for propositional logic (Wright 1967/1957a: 30).

There are, in fact, infinitely many topologically equivalent ways to diagram the truth tables of propositional logic directly (Gardner 1968: 56–57). Gardner devotes a chapter to a more iconic (Peirce's term for literally geometrical) network diagram for the propositional calculus using only lines (Gardner 1968: ch. 3). This is of practical interest because lines can be electrical wires. "That the propositional calculus can be translated into [computer circuit] network theory has been widely recognized for almost two decades" (Gardner 1968: 61). Englebretsen (1998), too, uses only line segments. Their chief antecedent is Johann Heinrich Lambert, who uses lines and dots to diagram the four categorical statements of syllogistic

(Englebretsen 1998: 15). Lambert uses line segments to diagram exclusive disjunction (Venn 1971/1894: 522, showing Lambert's diagram). Truth trees are essentially line diagrams, and line diagrams are essentially truth trees. But for any of these logics, the only question for us is whether in diagramming the premisses, we already diagram the conclusion of a valid argument.

The point about topological equivalence suggests the following argument that all logic diagrams are geometrical. (1) All logic diagrams are topological in the sense that if you draw a Venn diagram, Vennis ball, truth table, or truth tree on a rubber surface, the logical relationships will remain the same no matter how much you twist or turn the rubber (compare Gardner 1968: 28). (2) Topology is a branch of geometry. (3) Therefore all logic diagrams are geometrical. Of course, linguistic logics are geometrical in this sense too. In fact, any logic book can be written on rubber pages. And this is a big part of why linguistic and diagram logics are mutually rewritable. Namely, logical structure itself is topological in this sense.

Frege's formal logic is often seen as just such a blend or hybrid.[4] But no, it is a diagram logic pure and simple. It is a diagram logic because it is a positive truth tree logic. For you trace the positive flow of truth-grounds along the connecting lines in a proof. I did not see this until December 9, 2011. That is because Frege's formal logic is visually so unlike Jeffrey's negative truth trees (which close off paths of truth-flow that fail), not to mention Venn diagrams or Wittgenstein's truth tables. But what else could Frege's logic be? What else could its connecting lines be for, if not for showing truth-flow? And while it includes labels for statements or their logical components, so do Venn diagrams and truth tables. A labeled diagram is just that: a diagram with labels. This places Frege squarely in the logic diagram tradition. And since Frege was the founder of modern classical logic, it puts modern classical logic squarely in the logic diagram tradition from the start. In light of everything else discussed so far, this should be no surprise.

Unlike the relevance tradition they claim to champion, Anderson and Belnap never expressly diagram their own relevance logic. They never represent it by literally geometrical figures, and they seem unaware that truth tables and truth trees are diagrams at all. (Lattices do appear here and there in their volumes.) Indeed, in *Entailment*, volume 2, Alasdair Urquhart says:

> [O]ne of the main aims of this section is to make logicians aware of the rich possibilities offered by the techniques of classical synthetic geometry in the field of relevance logics....
>
> The connection between projective geometry and relevance logics is both simple and natural, and it makes sense to ask why it was not investigated earlier. (Urquhart 1992: 357)

This overlooks the forest for a tree. Geometrical diagrams were used by thousands of logicians for centuries to show *analytic* whole-part relevant containment. Again, we need not offer a geometric semantics, model, or interpretation for logical relevance here. The point is that diagrams are the traditional *test*, or *sufficient condition*, of containment and thus of entailment. If Anderson and Belnap do not see that even the humblest Venn diagram shows truth-ground containment if it shows a valid argument at all, no wonder they do not see how wrong their variable sharing requirement is. For the very tradition they champion makes a clear, direct, historical progression from literally geometrical figures through truth tables to truth trees, diagramming modus ponens and disjunctive syllogism as relevantly valid every step of the way. But Anderson and Belnap confine themselves to developing geometrical models of their own logic, most of which are too remote from ordinary intuition of whole-part inclusion even to *discover* except by specially written computer programs (Anderson 1992: 348–58). That does not speak well for their claim to be representing the mainstream tradition on relevant containment.

To sum up, the differences between the three main sorts of diagram make no difference. On any of them, we visibly show validity by diagramming the truth of the conclusion in the very act of diagramming the truth of the premisses. Whether or not they are purely or literally geometrical is moot.

Irving Anellis kindly suggests using "representation" in place of my "diagram," and using "diagram" in place of my "literally geometrical diagram." His intent to choose a neutral term is good. But this is moot: what counts is whether we diagram the conclusion in diagramming the premisses. It is also mere semantics; whatever term we use for the concept, Gardner's definition would be the same.

Of course, the concept of validity (impossibility of the conclusion's falsehood if the premisses are true), and the concept of relevant entailment (following from), are different concepts. The thesis is that they are logically equivalent. This gives us an *informative* analysis of validity as being relevant entailment, *pace* Wittgenstein's belief that logically equivalent statements express the same sense. I believe this was implicitly the traditional view. Anderson and Belnap accept it too, but they restrict validity to their limited kind of relevant entailment.[5]

Passing the traditional diagram test of entailment does not require meeting the Anderson-Belnap variable sharing requirement. Of course, Anderson and Belnap can always reject the traditional test because it fails to meet their variable sharing requirement. They can even quibble with the diagrams for this reason. But then the question arises whether they really follow or even understand the relevance tradition.

Anderson and Belnap say the "notion of relevance was central to logic from the time of Aristotle" (Anderson 1975: xxi). Have they noticed that Aristotelian syllogistic does not use Anderson-Belnap variable sharing? The categorical syllogism requires very different variable sharing. For example, the middle term must appear in both premises, and never in the conclusion.[6] But on every truth-ground containment test from Venn diagrams to truth trees, every valid Aristotelian syllogism correctly counts as valid. And on every rewrite of class inclusion in Aristotelian syllogistic as truth-ground containment, every valid class inclusion correctly counts as a truth-ground containment. And *only* they so count. And it is precisely the middle term that does the relevant linking:

> Premisses are *irrelevant* to their conclusions if one cannot find a valid syllogism to link them. And it is an unequivocal Middle Term that links the premises of a valid argument, the harbinger of Relevance. (Meyer 1985: 610)

Might not all and only valid Aristotelian syllogisms happen to be valid Anderson-Belnap tautological entailments anyway? No. For the Barbara syllogism and modern classical hypothetical syllogism are mutually rewritable (see Copi 1978: 229, citing Kant 1965/1787: A71/B96; see 1988/1800: 107). And as we saw at the beginning of this book, modern classical hypothetical syllogism is not a tautological entailment on the Anderson-Belnap definition (Anderson 1975: 157), even though visible containment of its conclusion in its premises can be directly diagrammed in all the ways we described. Nor is there any doubt that modern classical hypothetical syllogism is what we need to rewrite Barbara. For the premises of and conclusion of Barbara need not be tautological entailments themselves, as in Anderson-Belnap hypothetical syllogism (Anderson 1975: 160), but can be logically contingent. "All dogs are fish, all fish are stars, therefore all dogs are stars" is a perfectly valid Barbara. And where "s" is an object-name, "$((Dog(s) \supset Fish(s))$ and $(Fish(s) \supset Star(s))$, therefore $Dog(s) \supset Star(s)$" is a perfectly valid modern classical hypothetical syllogism. And as we saw, modus ponens and disjunctive syllogism can be rewritten as Barbara too! The reader can check the rest of Aristotle's categorical syllogisms, but I think the relevant Dog Star is enough.

Thus Aristotle is the implicit origin or logical root of modern classical extensional containment relevance, including modus ponens and disjunctive syllogism as well as hypothetical syllogism. The chief difference between Aristotelian and modern classical categorical syllogisms is merely that the latter remove existential import from universal quantification.

Of course, Anderson and Belnap are free to say that Aristotle is confused, that his Barbara syllogism is invalid, and that even its Venn diagram does not show relevant containment. But how convincing is that? And how traditional? Of course, categorical syllogistic does have *some* sort of variable sharing, even though it is not Anderson-Belnap's. We may say that Aristotelian categorical entailment has two conditions: (1) truth preservation and (2) Aristotelian variable sharing. I shall discuss condition (2) later.[7] But even on the level of condition (1), or truth-ground containment relevance alone, it appears that Sylvan is rather wild when he says that modern "classical logic is not in a privileged historical position. It is a rather recent upstart, a quite minor character" (Sylvan 2000: 133).

Aristotle was probably more interested in syllogistic classificatory science than in proof of new conclusions. One must not be confused here by the fact that truth-grounds are truth-possibilities, while classes are truth-conditions or truth-makers. The distinction is moot because the issue for relevance is not ontological primacy, but generality of logical containment, that is, logical primacy. Classes may be *ontologically* deeper than (prior to) truth-values. But truth-grounds are more general than classes with respect to premisses' containing conclusions, and are therefore *logically* deeper (prior to) classes. This is already implicit in Aristotle.

4. Was Russell an Express Relevantist?

I take it that conclusion (4) of our main argument, that modern classical logic is relevant, has now been established. But was, say, Russell an *express* relevantist? Did he diagram his logic, or care to? Or did he know that his logic *was* diagrammed, either by himself or by others, or that it could be? Here much depends on what a diagram is, and on what he took a diagram to be.

It is widely held that Russell rarely, if ever, uses diagrams to represent deductive arguments, or discusses the logic diagrams of others. Indeed, he rarely, if ever, uses *literally geometrical* diagrams. There are none in *Principles of Mathematics*, *Principia Mathematica*, or *Introduction to Mathematical Philosophy*, and none I have found in his most relevant collected papers (Russell 1994; 1993; 1990). But it does not follow from this that he does not use logic diagrams at all, since there are at least two other main kinds of logic diagrams: truth tables and truth trees. Let us take the three sorts of diagram in order.

Russell uses literally geometrical diagrams in mathematics and in dynamics (Russell 1994: plate facing 44; 1990: 30–34, 109, 341–45, 367–86, 487–89). On his logicist thesis, the mathematical diagrams are implicitly logic diagrams of logicized mathematics. He also diagrams relational facts and judgments (Russell 1993: 118, 186, 195, 196, 197, 200).[1] Russell might have known of literally geometrical diagrams for his logic from Copi. Russell says Copi was one of his "pupils of quite outstanding ability" (Russell 1987/1967: 459). But the first edition of Copi's book came out only in 1954. Of course, Russell knew of Peirce, and cites Peirce in *Principles*. Russell briefly lectured on non-Euclidean geometry in 1896 at Johns Hopkins University (Russell 1987/1967: 134), where Peirce had taught logic and mathematics; but Peirce had retired and moved to Milford PA in 1887. In any case, Russell knew very little about Peirce (Hawkins 1997), and almost certainly nothing about Peirce's diagrams. It is hard to believe that Russell did not know of Venn's or Euler's diagrams, if only because Venn was a famous English logician and Euler a famous mathematician. But in any case he does not use them. No doubt this is because he wants to logicize mathematics, not mathematicize logic.

Russell expressly endorses truth tables, as well as Wittgenstein's whole-part containment theory of deductive validity. In his introduction to Wittgenstein's *Tractatus*, Russell says:

[W]e arrive at an amazing simplification of the theory of inference....Wittgenstein is enabled to assert that...**if p follows from q the meaning of p is contained in the meaning of q,** from which of course it results that nothing can be deduced from an atomic proposition [except itself]. (Russell 1969/1922: xvi, my bold emphasis)

Clearly, Russell is well aware that Wittgenstein's truth tables diagram following from as containment of truth-grounds.

Eight years later, Russell repeats this endorsement in *The Analysis of Matter*:

What is the common quality of the propositions which can be deduced from the premisses of logic? The answer given by Wittgenstein in the *Tractatus Logico-Philosophicus* seems to me the right one. Propositions which form part of logic, or which can be proved by logic, are all *tautologies*—i.e. they show that different sets of symbols are different ways of saying the same thing, or that one set says part of what the other says.... (Russell 1954/1927: 172)

Of course, every valid inference corresponds to a tautological hypothetical proposition.[2] Russell also endorses C. I. Lewis's strict implication as being whole-part deductive inference (Russell 1954/1927: 199–200). Russell says much the same thing in *An Outline of Philosophy*:

> I think we may lay it down that, in mathematics, the conclusion
> always asserts merely the whole or part of the premisses, though
> usually in new language.... (Russell 1974/1927: 87; see 90)

Surely Russell is well aware that in these later publications, he is implicitly characterizing all his own earlier deductive logics, and deductive logic in general, as whole-part containment logic.

Russell probably did not know about truth trees. Jeffrey's book appeared three years before Russell's death. But Jeffrey says his "truth trees (one-sided semantic tableaux)" method has roots in Herbrand via "Beth's method of semantic tableaux" and in Smullyan "(from whom I borrowed the idea of one-sidedness which reduces tableaux to trees)" (Jeffrey 1967: vii–ix); Leblanc (1976: 48 n.2) tells a fairly similar story. The origin is actually more complex, and is best described as a community effort (Anellis 1990a). In any case, semantic tableaux and truth trees are basically just dressed-up truth tables. Thus the basic idea *behind* truth trees was familiar to Russell. And I can scarcely imagine that he would reject truth trees, since he accepts truth tables.

It is only barely possible that Russell heard of Lewis Carroll's falsifiability tree method for syllogisms. It was written in 1894, lost around 1900, eventually rediscovered, and published after Russell's death. See Bartley (1972); Carroll (1977/1896: Book 7); Anellis (1990; 1990a); Abeles (1990).

What does Russell take a diagram to be? I do not know. I am not sure he ever says. But even the question whether a truth table or truth tree is a diagram is moot. For what counts is the truth-ground containment. What counts is whether we represent the truth of a valid conclusion in the very act of representing the truth of the premises. And with respect to truth tables, clearly he knew *that*.

The three main functions of a logic diagram are proof, understanding entailment as containment by perceptibly (usually visually) representing it, and, at least where classes are diagrammed, aiding classificatory science by showing classificatory relationships. Of these three, understanding (intellectually seeing) the containment is primary, since here proof and classification are done (intellectually seen) *through* understanding (intellectually seeing) the containment. We may not even be interested in proof or classification if these are already obvious. Here Russell is interested in understanding and in proof through understanding, but not in classification. Truth tables implicitly can be used to classify, insofar as they are rewritable—and interpretable—as class diagrams; but Russell does not notice this.

Does Russell ever use the term "relevant" and its cognates? Yes, talk of relevance is scattered through his writings, but none or almost none of it concerns deductive logic.[3]

This concludes my discussion of whether Russell is an express relevantist. It seems clear that he is, at least concerning propositional logic, and at least by 1922. This is in sharp contrast to whether he is an express modal logician. It is clear that he never offers any express modal logics, and never says that his logic is a modal logic (Dejnožka 2003a; 1999). Russell does not offer an express relevance logic either, but he does expressly endorse Wittgenstein's view that deductive inference is a matter of containment and of following from. This substantially amounts to saying, and in any case implies, that his own formal deductive logic is a truth-ground containment relevance logic as well, since it too is truth-functional.

This also concludes my presentation of my main argument.[4]

5. Two Main Conceptions of Relevance

The modern classical and the relevantist conceptions of relevance lead to contradictory results. On the first view, modus ponens and disjunctive syllogism are relevantly valid. On the second view, they are not. I propose to apply the scholastic maxim, when faced with an apparent contradiction, draw a distinction. This is not the only way to handle an apparent contradiction. More generally, this is a dilemma; and we can go between the horns (in any number of ways), or impale ourselves on (that is, accept) either horn. But with so many good logicians on each side of such a basic question, it seems unwise to write off either side as simply wrong. Thus some mutual accommodation seems called for. I have at least seven antecedents who take some sort of accommodating approach. I cannot discuss their merits in detail, but I shall briefly state how I differ from each of them, after the following general remark.

One might think that relevantists as such cannot be ecumenical, since they say modern classical logic is bad *because* it is irrelevant; and that any ecumenicists could only be logicians who hold that modern classical validity as such is good, but that relevance can be interesting in special ways. This is in effect the line most of my antecedents take. But David Lewis and I hold that modern classical logic *is* relevant—extensionally relevant. This view may seem unique to us. But I believe it is implicit in every modern classical logician who uses truth tables, truth trees, or Venn diagrams to show validity. And I believe it is explicit in every modern classical logician who endorses Wittgenstein's express equation of truth-ground containment with following from. I proceed now to the seven antecedents of my view.

First, Russell himself, in his 1913 unpublished book manuscript *Theory of*

Knowledge, seems to assign relevance not to logic, but to epistemology (Russell 1993/1913: 50). In logic, the closest concept he admits is that of elegance (Russell 1993/1913: 50), which implies use-relevance insofar as it rejects unusable and unused premisses. Of course, unused premisses can be and are discarded even in modern classical logic; see Bolzano (1972/1837: § 155.26) on "*irredundant*" or "*precise*" deducibility. Briefly, I find it better to hold that there are two kinds of relevance in logic, extensional (truth-ground) and intensional, and that there is *also* epistemic (evidential) relevance in epistemology.

Second, Quine lived through the relevantist revolution and was criticized. Harold N. Lee says:

> By avoiding or denying status to intensions, Quine succeeds in omitting relevance itself. Relevance depends on intensional meanings. Two concepts are relevant insofar as they share intensional content; and two sentences are relevant insofar as they share conceptual content. (Lee 1986: 305)

In his reply to Lee, Quine confirms that he basically rejects intensions, but does not discuss relevance there (Quine 1986a). Elsewhere, Quine turns the relevantist attack back onto the relevantists, finding relevance basic to modern classical logic:

> The importance of implication is that it transmits truth. A falsehood will imply both truths and falsehoods, but a truth implies only truths....
>
> It is here that the logical forms are principally useful, for they depict features *relevant* to logical truth, suppressing *irrelevancies*. (Quine 1978: 40–41, my italic emphases)

I assume he means truth-ground relevance, since he holds that truth tables and even Venn diagrams show validity. As to the sort of implications relevantists like, Quine finds non-truth-functional subjunctive conditionals "important for the philosophy of science, for [they are] implicit in those terms of disposition or potential with which the sciences abound," but to have no use in logic or mathematics (Quine 1983: 16). That is, their proper *locus* is natural science, not logic. Except for my one quote of him on page 34, it never seems to occur to Quine that truth-ground containment *is* extensional logical relevance. Briefly, I prefer to locate both truth-ground and intensional relevance in logic, and to admit that there is *also* scientific relevance in science. (It may be that scientific relevance and logical relevance are species of epistemic relevance, but this is not my topic here.)

Anderson and Belnap are, of course, not interested merely in paraphrasing ordinary language conditionals into formal relevance logic. They also want to do this for the natural or empirical sciences and for mathematics. I question whether modern classical logic, perhaps constrained in various ways, would not be at least as viable; but this would take us too far afield. I can only note here that many philosophers of science and of mathematics, perhaps most, have been modern classical logicians; this includes Russell and Quine.

Third, M. Richard Diaz offers his own relevance logics based on three-valued truth tables. He suggests that such logics have definite but limited uses, and that deductive validity is usually all we need. Among other things, his core definition of truth-relevance validates disjunctive syllogism but not ex contradictione quodlibet sequitur (Diaz 1981: 67–68). Diaz's view is thoughtful, and is a sort of halfway house between Anderson-Belnap and Wittgenstein-Russell.

I agree with Diaz that "relevance logic is not, and should not be, the primary tool for logical studies," since in logic we are mainly interested in deductive proofs, and modern classical logic suffices for that (Diaz 1981: 9). I agree with him that relevantist logic is the most basic kind to study when intensional "relevance plays a crucial role" because "we are primarily interested in relevance relations" of the sort relevantists study, as "when we study the strength of assumptions, alternative foundations for systems, or the structure of proofs or systems" intensionally (Diaz 1981: 9). I also agree that "there may be various theories of [relevantist] relevance based on various (but perhaps similar) intuitive foundations" (Diaz 1981: 57). But it never occurs to Diaz that classical deductive validity might *be* whole-part relevant containment of truth-grounds.

Fourth, Meyer says that our "truth-functional intuitions" are "normally" the "preferable" ones (Meyer 1985: 598). Meyer says:

> Material ⊃ is an *integral* part of Relevant understanding, without which we will scarcely understand Relevant logics them-selves....[T]he amazing thing about these logics is not how much of the Material has been expunged, but how much of it has survived....
>
> Material ⊃ is a perfectly good particle of E. There are perfectly good theorems in it—all the material tautologies, to begin with. Whether we choose—in one particular inferential situation or another—to follow the properly relevant recommendations of E, or the merely Material ones, is our business....And one thing that a formal system *cannot* do is to specify the conditions of its application.
>
> So, instead of a ceaseless "paradigm clash" between Relevant and Material insights, one has the opportunity to reconcile these insights. If Material logic is not so much wrong as crude, we can avail ourselves of its crudities, without being bound by them when they lead to Trouble. (Meyer 1985: 598; see 604–606)

Thus Meyer makes a "plea for rapprochement" (Meyer 1985: 632). One may ask rapprochement with what, since he rejects the very possibility of a concept of entailment. Is that not inconsistent? But he merely thinks that no one logic can be "the" relevance logic, and that there are many relevance insights to be had. Meyer's paper is a fine one. But he does not see that modern classical logic is extensionally relevant. And I think his farewell to entailment was premature, at least in the sense that the literature is flourishing. I think it flourishes precisely because of the variety of insights which Meyer says leads to "diminishing returns" (1985: 618). I myself list fourteen senses of "relevant" in my (1999: 166). Far from destroying the subject to be investigated, it is this very richness that makes it interesting. In fact, if we never investigated rich and complex subjects, we would never investigate much of anything. I myself see the question whether there is any single best relevance logic as posterior to the more interesting, more general question raised by the journal *Logica Universalis*: Can all or at least most logics be integrated into one? For me, this would include modern classical logic as the basic ingredient in an integration of relevance logics. And at least in principle, there can be objective evaluation of the many relevance logics. This would include their capacities to paraphrase, to avoid paradoxes, and so on.

Fifth, Georg Schurz and Paul Weingartner propose using relevant consequence classes to "rehabilitate" Karl Popper's thesis that the theory that is closest to the truth (has the most truth-likeness or verisimilitude) is the one that "has more true consequences and less false ones than the other alternative theories" Schurz (1987: 47). This is a fine approach. But they do not see that Popper's notion is already truth-ground relevant containment, to which they are merely adding additional relevantist constraints. For Popper says his notion of verisimilitude:

combin[es] two notions, both originally introduced by Tarski: (a) the notion of *truth*, and (b), the notion of the (logical) *content* of a statement; that is, the class of all statements logically entailed by it (its "consequence class," as Tarski usually calls it).... (Popper 1979/1972: 47, citing Tarski 1956 (1st ed.): essay 7; see Popper 2007/1963: 315–20, 527–35; Tarski 1983 (2d ed.): essays 3, 5, 7)

The idea of importance to us is that two statements have the same content if and only if they have the same consequence classes. In effect, this equates content containment with following from. I cannot discuss Popper or Tarski here; besides Schurz (1987), see Gemes (2007). But I wish to note that Tarski's (or Popper's) notion (b) already occurs in Frege. This has been raised as the question whether, for Frege, logically equivalent statements express the same thought (sense). Dummett and I agree that they do not (Dejnožka 2007: 68–69); the notorious texts are Frege (1970/1892b: 46 n.*; 1970/1894a: 80). Of course, Frege's senses, as opposed to his customary references, are intensional, so this would not affect extensionalist relevant containment for Frege. See page 111 and Dejnožka (2007: 60–62) on the four main modern classical senses of "intension" and "extension." Only logically equivalent statements' *constituent names* can refer to different references for Frege; his statements are always names of truth-values. But it is the early Frege, who has an undifferentiated notion of propositional content not yet split into sense and reference, who clearly states Tarski's (or Popper's) notion (b). Frege says in a famous text in *Begriffsschrift*:

A distinction between *subject* and *predicate* does *not occur* in my way of representing a judgment....[T]he contents of two judgments may differ in two ways: either the consequences derivable from the first, when it is combined with certain other judgments, always follow also from the second, [and conversely,] or this is not the case. The two propositions, "The Greeks defeated the Persians at Plataea" and "The Persians were defeated by the Greeks at Plataea" differ in the first way. Now I call that part of the content that is the same in both the *conceptual content*. Since *it alone* is of significance for our ideography, we need not introduce any [ordinary grammatical subject-predicate] distinction between propositions having the same conceptual content. [I]n a judgment I consider only that which influences its *possible* consequences. (Frege 1977/1879: 12, his emphasis; compare 1970/1892b: 46 n.*, quoted in part below)

This, I submit, is the first statement of extensionalist relevant containment in the analytic tradition. For Frege is expressly defining "conceptual content" as being "that part of the content that is the same in both;" and what is the same in both is precisely having the same *consequences*. Note that Frege is not describing the nature of conceptual content (is not offering a theoretical definition), much less arguing for it, but is merely stipulating what is to be called conceptual content, in accord with his sole interest in inference.

Five years later, Frege makes the second statement of deduction as containment in the analytic tradition, in *Grundlagen*:

[In deduction n]ew propositions must be derived from [the premisses] which are not contained in any one of them by itself. No doubt these propositions are in a way contained covertly in the whole set [of premisses] taken together, but this does not absolve us from the labour of actually extracting them and setting them out in their own

40   The Concept of Relevance and the Logic Diagram Tradition

right. (Frege 1974/1884: 23)

Frege even repeats the point, this time for deriving propositions from definitions:

> Often we need several definitions for the proof of some proposition,
> which consequently is not contained in any one of them alone, yet
> does follow purely logically from all of them taken together. (Frege
> 1974/1884: 101)

In this passage, we see not only deduction as containment, but its apparent equation with "follow[ing] from" (Frege's term), and apparently a relevant use or "need" (Frege's term) requirement as well.

I shall now make my promised return to the topic of Aristotelian variable sharing. This is the deeper level on which Schurz and Weingartner are my fifth antecedent. For they include what they call Aristotelian relevance in the relevance criterion they use to rehabilitate Popper (Schurz 1987: 55 citing Weingartner 1986). Thus their "relevance criterion...entails [Aristotelian] A-relevance" (Schurz 1987: 70). In a later paper on Aristotle's logic, Weingartner speaks of relevantist filters. He means that relevantist criteria weaken modern classical logic in that they limit what can be proved by strengthening what implication requires. He correctly notes of categorical syllogisms that the middle term never appears in the conclusion, but that no term appears in the conclusion that does not appear in the premisses. (The major term is always in the major premiss, and the minor term in the minor.) Thus syllogistic has variable sharing, but not of the sort Anderson and Belnap require. That "the conclusion must not contain predicates which do not already appear in one of the premisses," and thus "is not richer than the premisses," is Aristotelian or "A-relevance" (Weingartner 1994: 99–100). The "A-criterion" applies A-relevance only to the main conditional connective of an inference in propositional logic. "A-restricted valid formulas" include modus ponens and disjunctive syllogism, but not ex contradictione quodlibet (Weingartner 1994: 102). The "A*-criterion" applies A-relevance to all the conditional connectives in an inference in propositional logic, that is, to all the conditional connectives *within* each premiss and the conclusion as well as to the main one. This universal application is closer to Anderson-Belnap entailment, but it also achieves closure under modus ponens, which the A-criterion did not do. For example, $(p \ \& \ q) \to p$ and $((p \ \& \ q) \to p) \to (\neg p \to \neg(p \ \& \ q))$, therefore $\neg p \to \neg(p \ \& \ q)$ is an instance of modus ponens which is A*-closed under modus ponens, but not A-closed, since only the conclusion violates A, but both the second premiss and the conclusion violate A* (Weingartner 1994: 103, 105). (Closure means that if all the premisses meet the criterion, then so does a valid conclusion, i.e., that when an operation of valid inference is applied to members of the set of statements that meet the criterion, the resulting valid conclusion is always a member of the set too.) Weingartner says that all this can be extended to quantificational logic by rewriting (1994: 119 n.27), and argues that Aristotelian relevance helps avoid various paradoxes. See also Weingartner (1985: 563–75). All this is fine as far as it goes. But Weingartner, like his respondent Suppes (1994), does not realize that modern classical logic is already truth-ground containment relevant, so that Aristotelian (or any other) relevantist filters merely add extra forms of relevance to it. In fact, Schurz and Weingartner insist that the opposite is the case:

> [I]t is simply not our aim to construct a "new logic[,"] but we *remain* in *classical* logic and use our relevance criterion only as a *filter* singling out the relevant valid implications from the set of all (relevant or irrelevant) valid implications. We want to strongly emphasize that we distinguish clearly [and extensionally] between

relevance and validity. (Schurz 1987: 55)

Thus they oppose relevance to modern classical logic, specifically to modern classical validity.

Sixth, Greg Restall defines worlds as maximal consistent sets of states, and finds that modern classical logic is the appropriate logic for worlds, and relevance logic is the appropriate logic for states (Restall 1999: 66–67). He says that "relevant logics....are designed to give us 'finer' notions of validity and of conditionality, and they do this through the use of the finely individuated states, over and above the coarse worlds" (Restall 1999: 67). Thus we have classical validity understood in terms of worlds, and relevant validity understood in terms of states. He then says:

> This explains the validity of disjunctive syllogism. *It is valid in the weak sense that whenever a world makes the premises true, then that world (of necessity) also makes the conclusion true.* This does not mean that the corresponding conditional is relevantly valid....But both sorts of validity have their place, and both can coexist, as can be seen by our models. The *more fundamental* sort requires truth preservation across all states. The second, *less discriminating* kind of validity requires only truth preservation across all worlds. (Restall 1999 67–68, my italic emphases)

I have only two criticisms of this brilliant account. First, Restall does not see that classical validity is whole-part truth-ground relevant containment. The closest he comes to seeing this is in the complete sentence I italicized. Second, even though Restall defines worlds as certain special sets of states, it is modern classical validity that is more fundamental. For to say it is less discriminating is precisely to say it is the genus, and relevantist validity is a species.

Restall says ecumenically,

> Truth preservation across all states differs from truth preservation across all worlds. Truth is preserved in the step from A & $(\neg A \vee B)$ to B when we evaluate the formulae at worlds, but not when we evaluate the formulae at all states. Both are fine notions for logical study, and both have some correlation to our pretheoretic notion of validity. (Restall 1999: 69)

Restall then comes very close to my own genus-species view by saying:

> The whole account is not so much a rival to classical logic as an extension to it. It extends classical logic with a new relation of validity, which respects the canons of relevance by considering states. According to this conception, there are (at least) two notions of validity, and each has their own use. (Restall 1999: 69)

Restall says more recently:

> [I]t is impossible that the premises of an instance of disjunctive syllogism be true if at the very same time the conclusion is not true. Relevant entailment is not the *only* constraint under which truth may be regulated. Relevant entailment is one useful criterion for evaluating reasoning. If we are given reason to believe $A \vee B$ and reason to believe $\neg A$, then (provided those reasons do not conflict with one another) we have reason to believe B. The reason is not one

licensed by relevant consequence, but relevant consequence is not the only sort of licen[s]e to which a good inference might aspire. (Restall 2006: 316)

But he thinks the genus is validity and the difference is relevance, while I think the genus is relevance in the sense of truth-ground containment and the difference is relevantist (or intensional) validity. If I am right, this answers the question, Which basic kind of relevance is logically prior? For truth-ground containment is the genus, and relevantist logics are species. And a genus is logically prior to its species. Granted, things can often be classified differently. For an old example, we can take rational as genus and animal as difference, making humans and angels mutually exclusive species of the same genus. But this is not one of those cases, at least if relevantist proofs are a proper sub-class of modern classical proofs.

Seventh, David Lewis basically shares my view, but is closer to Restall in general approach. Where Restall uses states, Lewis uses "subject matters" or "parts of the world in intension" (Lewis 1988: 162). I imagine I could use my qualified facts (see Dejnožka 2003: xxvi, 47, 61, 73, 123–35 on qualified objects) in place of states or subject matters, even though that is a different conception arising out of phenomenological issues. (A qualified object is an object as conceived or regarded in a certain manner, but such that there can be no object in itself, so that there can be veridical, illusory, and even delusory qualified objects. Antoine Arnauld's notion of a qualified thing is an antecedent.) But I chose to discuss diagrams here, not qualified worlds. Lewis argues in effect that truth preserving validity is always relevant in the sense of truth-ground overlap or containment (Lewis 1988). The Lewis-Restall approach is also similar to the early Wittgenstein's. The notion of possible worlds, or of totalities of existing and nonexisting atomic states of affairs, states, or subject matters, is deeply related to that of truth table matrices of truth-possibilities. Restall mainly differs from Lewis on modal realism (Restall 1999).

Perhaps Restall's, Lewis's, and my own dualistic conceptions can be diagrammed in terms of filing systems, following Thomas V. Morris's use of filing systems to explain Frege's use of the sense-reference distinction to explain informative identity statements (Morris 1984). Here Restall's states, Lewis's subject matters or parts of the world in intension, and my qualified facts would equate to senses; my qualified objects are expressly intended to replace senses. In any case, the two concepts of relevance seem to call for a dualistic conception of logic and of meaning. But Wittgenstein seems to tie sense to reference too tightly for this to work as one might hope.

This concludes my survey of seven antecedents of my view that modern classical validity is the primary form of relevant entailment and there are secondary, more restrictive forms. Only one of the seven, Lewis, agrees with me that modern classical validity *is* relevant entailment. Of course, Wittgenstein and the 1921 Russell are antecedents simpliciter of my view that modern classical validity is truth-ground containment. And Russell, Wright, and Geach impose an epistemic or practical filter or constraint on modern classical validity so as to achieve a more restricted sort of relevant entailment; I shall discuss that later.

I come now to my own view. I agree with Sylvan that the core area is semantics. Sylvan says, "The paradoxes of implication are paradoxical because of semantical features, the semantics of implication especially" (Sylvan 2000: 40). For Sylvan, the core issue is validity. Fallacies of relevance "bear directly on validity" (Sylvan 2000: 40). But semantics concerns both intension and extension. I hold that Wittgenstein states the extensional semantics of propositional logic correctly and shows its validity. Yet we cannot say that Wittgenstein therefore rejects intensions. He says, "A thought is a proposition with a sense" (T 4; see 5.122 quoted earlier). Frege and Russell, too, distinguish intension from extension.

Anderson and Belnap say:

Indeed the Official position [of modern classical logic] is that the only right-minded attitude is to shrug off the concept of relevance by asserting dogmatically that "...the notion of connection or dependence being appealed to here is too vague to be a formal concept of logic" (Suppes 1957), or by asking rhetorically, "How is one to characterize such an obscure notion as that of [logical] dependence?

We, on the contrary, take the question at face value and offer two formal conditions, the first as necessary and sufficient [possibility of use in a proof as shown by subscripting], the second as necessary only [variable sharing]. (Anderson 1975: 30)[21]

That may be the official position of Suppes, Anderson, and Belnap. But it is scarcely the position of the early Wittgenstein, Russell, or Quine, since they offer a perfectly sharp and clear "necessary and sufficient" "formal condition" of logical "'connection or dependence'," namely, truth-ground containment.

Anderson and Belnap find sharing of "meaning content" or "intensional meaning" to be intuitively correct as far as it goes, and only needing adequate formalizing as variable sharing (Anderson 1975: 32–33; 152–55; compare 176–77). They say their view opposes that of "the extensional community" (Anderson 1975: 36), and sails against "the prevailing Extensional Winds" (Anderson 1975: 256). They say variable sharing "concerns...logical consequence, and is semantical in character" (Anderson 1975: 33). They say subscripting "has to do with entailment...as the converse of deducibility, and in this sense is...proof-theoretical" (Anderson 1975: 33; see 186 on syntactics and semantics). I hold that truth-grounds concern both deducibility and logical consequence at once. Where deduction is formal proof by syntactical rules, and logical consequence is semantic derivability of truth-value, they are the two sides of the coin of proof by truth table. For a truth table is a syntactical matrix of semantic truth-values.

Anderson and Belnap say of variable sharing, "If this property fails,...then the resulting propositions have no meaning content in common and are totally irrelevant to each other" (Anderson 1975: 33). This is a non sequitur. They overlook truth-ground containment, or *truth-ground sharing*. Perhaps this is partly because they also overlook that their favorite expressions, "meaning content," "information content," and "semantic content," are ambiguous as to intensional or extensional.

Anderson and Belnap say it is precisely because relevance is so closely tied to intensionality that logicians have thought it *"impossible"* to treat formally (Anderson 1975: xxi–xxii, their emphasis). And they say this is precisely why they take a humble, nuts and bolts extensional approach (Anderson 1975: xxii). Yet bewitched by their picture of relevance as intensional, they are unable to see the truth-ground containment relevance of $(A \ \& \ \neg A \ ) \rightarrow B$ (Anderson 1975: 151–52).

Others are bewitched too. Ross Brady says "the following [are] desirable principles":

(e1) No truth-functional wff is part of the [intensional] meaning of every statement.

(e2) No truth-functional wff includes in its [intensional] meaning every statement.

(e3) No tautology is part of the [intensional] meaning of every statement.

(e4) No contradiction includes in its [intensional] meaning every statement.

(e5) For truth functional A and B, B is included in the [intensional] meaning of A only if B shares a sentential parameter with A. (Brady 2003: 216, italic emphases removed)

Now, these principles are correct, and (e5) is especially insightful, for relevantist logic. But it is a non sequitur to say there is anything wrong with modern classical logic. For (e1)–(e5) concern intensional meaning, while truth-ground relevance concerns extensional meaning. I doubt any modern classical logician has ever said that the *intension* of "1 + 1 = 2" is a logical part of the *intension* of "Snow is white;" and if any did, s/he was wrong. Yet the *truth-grounds* of the latter contain the *truth-grounds* of the former. Thus Brady's principles are consistent with these further principles:

(e*1) The truth-grounds of some truth-functional wffs are included (contained) in the truth-grounds of every statement.

(e*2) The truth-grounds of some truth-functional wffs include the truth-grounds of every statement.

(e*3) The truth-grounds of every tautology are included in the truth-grounds of every statement.

(e*4) The truth-grounds of every contradiction include the truth-grounds of every statement.

(e*5) For truth functional A and B, if the truth-grounds of A are included in the truth-grounds of B, then B may but need not share a sentential parameter with A.

Thus Wittgenstein is right "that arguments to the basic paradoxes of strict implication simply show that necessary and impossible statements *are* connected to everything else" (Sylvan 2000: 38), namely, by truth-ground containments; though in a deeper sense they are not connected to *anything* else, or more accurately, to anything real; see T 5.142, 5.143 on tautology and contradiction. Nor does this mean that "demonstrations could be truncated, since any necessary truth yields any other" (Sylvan 2000: 61), due to a forward constraint which I shall explain later.

The elegance of the modern classical logicians is to see that once we focus on truth-grounds, ordinary intensional relevance drops out of the picture as, well, irrelevant. Of course, the relevantists want truth preservation *too*, but they want something more intensional, more intuitive. This helps explain why for relevantists, relevance is such a delicate matter, and why they disagree with each other so much, while for modern classical logicians, relevance is basically mechanical and there is very little disagreement.

Actually, logic divides into syntax, intensional and extensional semantics, and *pragmatics*. Sylvan accepts syntactic, "semantic and pragmatic connection of components of genuine implications" (Sylvan 2000: 37). See also Pietarinen (2005) comparing Peirce to Dan Sperber and Deirdre Wilson on relevance and contextual meaning. Pragmatic relevance is the other main relevantist species of modern classical logic, on pain of otherwise admitting pragmatic inferences where all the premisses are true, yet the conclusion can be false.

6. Objections

William of Ockham says, "The ability of a doctrine to handle objections is a sign of its truth" (Ockham 1974/1323: 84). Or better, its inability to handle them is a sign of its falsehood.

First, there are several traditional general objections to modeling proofs with diagrams at all: "1. diagrams represent individual cases[, so that it is hard to know how far they can be safely generalized] 2. often they are misleading[,] 3. they are just heuristic tools, helpful from a psychological and pedagogical point of view," but not rigorous or "mathematical" (!) (Magnani 2001: 204). But as we have already seen, Shin (1994: ch. 3) shows that a diagram logic can be just as rigorous and well-defined as a linguistic logic. Even Magnani finds that diagrams can be more than merely heuristic, citing several formal logic diagrams (Magnani 2001: 204–5).

Second, there is a specific objection to diagramming disjunctive syllogism from within the modern classical camp itself. Englebretsen praises Shin (1994) for developing "a purely diagrammatic approach to logic" (Englebretsen 1998: 11). But Shin herself argues that no diagram for disjunctive syllogism can be purely iconic, since disjunction itself cannot be pictured. For disjunction is not part of what is, and thus is not there to be pictured. Shin concludes that disjunction cannot be literally diagrammed, but only added as a conventional linguistic element to a diagram logic. The argument is that there can be no photograph or picture of alternative possibilities, but only of what is. For example, we can see that the cat is on the mat, and we can photograph that, but we cannot see that the cat is either on the mat or in its basket, except insofar as we see it is on the mat. (Shin 1994: 180–84). This is not a new view. Russell repeatedly denies that we are acquainted with disjunction (Russell 1971/1918: 209–10; 1976/1948: 127; see also Black 1970: 220). This also affects modus ponens, both indirectly through its equivalence to disjunctive syllogism, and directly, since material implication is not a perceptible part of what is either. Thus both argument forms must use conventional linguistic elements for their main logical operators.[1]

Shin does not see this as a problem. She says, "As Peirce admits, sometimes one sign might belong to more than one category, or the distinction among them is not clear in some cases" (Shin 2002: 23); compare Shimojima (2001: 5–27), Stenning (2001: 32), and Cheng (2001: 84–85). She says, "For many reasons, we cannot [always] perfectly depict the situation we reason about, and we do not need to, either" (Shin 2002: 27). She quotes Peirce as saying merely that "'A diagram ought to be as iconic as possible'" (Shin 2002: 31). She says, "Moreover, the mixture of symbols and icons is not only theoretically possible, but more desirable than the 'purity' of homogeneous systems, since each kind of symbol has its own strengths and weaknesses" (Shin 2002: 172; compare Barwise 1994 on hyperproof). I agree with Shin.[2]

But even if Shin were wrong, it would not affect the relevant validity of these inference forms in her diagram logics in the least. The iconicity of logical operators is moot. For the test of relevant containment is not whether a diagram is purely geometrical or iconic, but whether we already represent the conclusion when we represent the premisses. Thus Shin is still able to say, "in the Alpha system we *see* logical equivalence" (Shin 2002: 97, Shin's emphasis), regardless of whether any logical operator is iconic at all.

Further, even if Shin is right that disjunction cannot be seen, she is conflating *what we see* with *what there is*, begging the question against disjunction as an abstract entity. It is a non sequitur to think that a part of a diagram is conventional because what it represents is imperceptible or even unreal. Nor does it matter whether what the diagram represents is part of the world as opposed to mere thought or mere language. Indeed, we ordinarily think that no thought is spatial at all, yet we have diagrammed them for centuries. Even if *all*, *none*, and classes are logical fictions, as they are for Russell, that would not prevent us from using Venn circles to represent them. And I see no reason why merely rational or linguistic items, including logical connectors, cannot be nonconventionally, geometrically represented *by analogy* to their logical or classificatory features. Again, the whole issue of iconicity or literal geometricality is moot. What counts is whether we diagram the conclusion in the very act of diagramming the premisses. It is simply irrelevant to this whether some parts of the diagram are conventional as opposed to geometrical. And it is just as irrelevant whether what the diagram represents is perceptible or real. Indeed, that is a rare question to be asking about *logic* diagrams!

Third, Sylvan says disjunctive syllogism is wrong because "if both A and $\neg A$ are assumed, then A cannot also be used to knock out $\neg A$ in $A \lor B$ [sic?] to arrive at B" (Sylvan 2000: 50). This is a red herring. If we use a truth table or other diagram, we are not assuming both A and $\neg A$ to be true. We are not assuming a contradiction to be true. We are not assuming anything to be true. We are diagramming all the truth-possibilities without any regard for the actual or assumed truth of any statement. But perhaps Sylvan really applies this reason to reject the following argument for ex contradictione quodlibet, which argument is *based on* disjunctive syllogism: If A & $\neg A$, then from A, it follows that $A \lor B$; then from $\neg A$ and $A \lor B$, it follows that B (Sylvan 2000: 111). But this too is a red herring. We can simply look at the truth table or other diagram for a direct observation of containment validity without all of this arguing from step to step.

Fourth, Anderson and Belnap, reading $A \to (B \to A)$ as saying that B implies A providing that A is true, argue that if A is contingent and B is necessary, then "we have a necessity entailing a contingency" (Anderson 1975: 14), which is absurd because necessary truths can only entail necessary truths, since "true entailments are necessarily so" (Anderson 1975: 14; see 12–13). But this is necessary *B* entailing contingent *A* in the consequent only because contingent *A* is already *given* or *assumed* to be true, so to speak, in the antecedent. This is the only reason why there is truth-ground containment here. Strictly speaking, if *A* is contingent, we have a contingency entailing a contingency. For if *A* is contingent, then so is $(B \to A)$, if *B* is necessary. There is a world of difference between necessary *B* entailing contingent *A* *in the consequent of a conditional whose antecedent is A*, and necessary *B* entailing contingent *A* simply or per se. In modern classical logic, the former is valid, the latter is not. In modern classical logic, $A \supset (B \supset A)$ is a tautology, $(B \supset A)$ by itself is not.

Anderson and Belnap also say that a contingent statement does not imply a necessary one (Anderson 1975: 36; see 12–13). This is their criticism of modern classical $A \to (B \to A)$, where *B* is contingent and *A* is necessary. Apparently they skip the proviso, "providing that *A* is true," that is, providing that the antecedent *A* is true, possibly reasoning that if *A* is necessary, then *A* must be true in any event. My reply is basically the same, except that here we have strictly speaking a necessity entailing a necessity. For if A is necessary, then so is $(B \to A)$, if *B* is contingent (and indeed, regardless of whether *B* is contingent). There is a world of difference between contingent *B* entailing necessary *A* *in the consequent of a conditional whose antecedent is A*, and contingent *B* entailing necessary *A* simply or per se. In modern classical logic, the former is valid, the latter is not.

Anderson and Belnap grant that the truth of "Crater Lake is blue" implies its possible truth, since actuality implies possibility. But they hold it cannot imply its necessary possibility (Anderson 1975: 38–39). They overlook that a necessary statement has no extensional content, and is thus contained by default in the extensional content of any statement that does have content. It might help to explain this in possible worlds talk. To say the lake is blue is to say it is blue in the actual world. To say that it is possibly blue is to say it is blue in *some* possible world, which is to say less. To say that if it is possibly blue, then it is necessarily possibly blue is to say that if it is blue in *some* possible world, then necessarily it is blue in *that* possible world. And that is because, following Leibniz, its being blue in that possible world is part of what defines or sets up that possible world. Or better, in a truth table, a possible statement, or statement that is true in at least one row, is *necessarily true in that row* simply because that is how the truth table is set up.

Fifth, Mares says "the standard notion of validity...allows too many non-sequiturs to be classified as good arguments" (Mares 2004: 3). But this is vague. For there is a paradox of the heap here: how many is "too many"? Many useful and important systems have built-in surds. The modern classical logicians were well aware of theirs, but proceeded and achieved their goals. No doubt relevantists consider modern classical logic to have many big surds. But surds are relative to point of view. Indeed, the bigger surd of the relevantists is their overlooking that truth-ground containment is relevant containment. At the least, Mares' considering these inferences to be surds begs the question against modern classical logic, on which some of them are truth-ground containments and others are constrained.

Sixth, no doubt Anderson and Belnap would object that the truth-ground diagrams of modern classical logic are flawed precisely because they fail to require variable sharing, that is, precisely because modus ponens and disjunctive syllogism pass the diagram test. Perhaps they would think that all such diagrams beg the question by being drawn so that modus ponens and disjunctive syllogism pass the test. But we are free to set up our logics any way we can, so as to show whatever we can. This freedom of stipulation is simply any logician's freedom to create new definitions and new representations. This includes diagram logics as well as linguistic logics. It seems to me that Venn, Peirce, Wittgenstein, Copi, Gardner, Jeffrey, and Shin drew their diagrams fair and square. Thus the burden is on

Anderson and Belnap to explain why all these diagrams, which appear for all the world to show truth-ground containment in the most visible and obvious way, do not show relevant containment at all. And this is just what they try to do in the case of Jeffrey trees for modern classical logic (Anderson 1992: 195–97). But they overlook the main argument of this book. And surely it is their view which begs the question against the traditional diagram test of entailment, and which ignores the visible obviousness of diagrams' showing containment of the conclusion in the premises.

Seventh, Anderson and Belnap say "most contemporary logicians somewhat" treat things as follows:

> The two-valued propositional calculus sanctions [many intuitively valid principles]; it consequently suggests itself as a candidate for a formal analysis of "if...then—" (Anderson 1975: 3)

Thus they claim that modern classical logicians are in the business of formally analyzing ordinary "if-then." They then proceed to find the supposed modern classical analysis perverse. They say that material implication and strict implication are not just "'odd kinds'" of implication, they are not "'kinds' of implication at all" (Anderson 1975: 4). They propose other names which are "no more 'misleading'," such as "material conjunction" or even "immaterial negation" (Anderson 1975: 5).

Many relevantists accuse modern classical logic of failing to formalize "if" correctly. Their arguments are subtle and impressive (see e.g. Anderson 1975: 17; Read 1988: 23–31, 23 n.2 citing Cooper 1968: 297, example 2.1; Mares 2004: 11–16). Anderson and Belnap even accuse modern classical logicians of "pretending to believe that [they mean material implication or even] $\neg A \lor B$ by "if A then B" (Anderson 1975: 329). They present an example of someone who argues that since no signal can travel faster than the speed of light, it follows in modern classical logic that "If every signal has a maximum velocity, then there is a maximum velocity which no signal exceeds" (Anderson 1975: 329). They report Charles L. Stevenson's example of someone who argues that if it is false that "If God exists then there is evil in the world," then "it follows that God exists and there is no evil in the world, thus (as Stevenson remarks) 'dismissing atheism and pessimism in one fell swoop'" (Anderson 1975: 330). That is, if $\neg(A \supset B)$, then $(A$ & $\neg B)$. This is a brilliant example of relevantists at their most persuasive. Indeed, the truth table for material implication shows the formal validity of the inference. And it is hard to call this a problem of paraphrase. How else could one paraphrase it? Of course, one can find the assumption false, and find it true (or at least possible) that (even) if God exists, then there is (or can still be) evil in the world. Many theologians do, often due to issues like temptation, sin, free will, love, forgiveness, mercy, humility, hope, or even simply learning submission to God's will. But finding the assumption false for theological reasons is totally irrelevant to the question, which is about the logical validity of the argument. That is, the suggested response substitutes soundness for validity.

One reply to the issue of material implication would be a tu quoque. If it is anyone Anderson and Belnap *sympathize* with, then they say, "if he wishes to speak in the way he does, who are we to complain?" (Anderson 1975: 332). They even defend *themselves* from the charge of ungrammaticality, specifically, the accusation of confusing object-language and meta-language, in their Grammatical Propaedeutic at the end of their first volume (Anderson 1975: xxiii). There, under the heading, "Reading formal constructions into English" (Anderson 1975: 486), they say about one question of formal paraphrase that goes against their views, "What follows? We think: nothing. We think this is a *sheer* grammatical fact about English, having no philosophical significance" (Anderson 1975: 487, their emphasis) They say in defense of themselves, though not at all in defense of modern classical logicians, all of whom hold the same view they do:

> [T]he structure of English may turn out to be a bad source for intuitions guiding the construction of a fruitful theory of truth, [and English grammar] should not dictate how we apply logical grammar. (Anderson 1975: 485)
>
> [I]t is not required that we slavishly take the details of English grammar as a sure guide to the most fruitful way to proceed. (Anderson 1975: 486; see also 488, 491)

Frege, Russell, the early Wittgenstein, and Quine would be the first to agree. Indeed, they pioneered the point. Frege explains his reasons for preferring a formal logical notation to ordinary language as early as his 1879 *Begriffsschrift* (Frege 1977/1879: 5–8), and repeatedly to the end of his life. Russell explains his reasons for the same preference in *Principia Mathematica* (Whitehead 1978/1910: 1–3), and champions formal logical notation against ordinary language philosophy in general as late as *My Philosophical Development* (Russell 1985/1959: ch. 18). The early Wittgenstein says "all the propositions of our everyday language, just as they stand, are in perfect logical order" (T 5.5563). But he is no ordinary language philosopher. He says "the reason why [the problems of philosophy] are posed is that the logic of our language is misunderstood" (Wittgenstein 1969/1921: 3). He says, "It is not humanly possible to gather immediately from" everyday language what its logical order is (T 4.002). He says, "Language disguises thought. So much so, that from the outward form of the clothing it is impossible to infer the form of the thought beneath it" (T 4.002). He expressly follows Frege and Russell in requiring a formal notation:

T 3.323 In everyday language it very frequently happens that the same word has different modes of signification—and so belongs to different symbols—or that two words that have different modes of signification are employed in propositions in what is superficially the same way....

T 3.325 In this way the most fundamental confusions are easily produced....

T 3.325 In order to avoid such errors we must make use of a sign-language that excludes them... that is to say, a sign-language that is governed by *logical* grammar—by logical syntax.

(The conceptual notation of Frege and Russell is such a language...)

Quine explains his preference for formal logical notation in *Word and Object*, in a chapter entitled "Aims and Claims of Regimentation" (Quine 1975/1960: ch. 33).

Perhaps all four of these great analysts might agree with Anderson and Belnap's final point:

We summarize the spirit of this Propaedeutic [as follows]: learn logical grammar thoroughly, and then—but only then—be relaxed about it. (Anderson 1975: 492)

I only wish Anderson and Belnap would apply the same generous spirit to their imagined opponents that they do to themselves. Instead, they say that violating ordinary usage is perfectly all right when it comes to their own logic, yet they criticize modern classical logicians for their "perversity" in violating ordinary usage (Anderson 1975: 5).

A second and deeper reply is that the relevantists are not the only ones who can claim some support from our ordinary logical intuitions. Consider this conversation: Smith: "How do you know that B?" Jones: "Well, I know that A is true, and I know that if A is true, then B is true." Smith: "But that knowledge is totally irrelevant to knowing that B. How can you say you know B on that basis?" Or consider this one: Smith: "How do you know that B?" Jones: "Well, I know that A or B is true, and I know that A is false." Smith: "But that is totally irrelevant to knowing that B. How can you say you know B on that basis?" Or consider a third conversation: Smith: "How do you know that if A then C?" Jones: "Well, I know that if A then B, and I know that if B then C." Smith: "But that is totally irrelevant to knowing that if A then C. How can you say you know if A then C on that basis?" Surely Smith's rejoinders are rather wild in every conversation.

The modus ponens conversation might continue: Smith: "But relevantists tell us modus ponens is invalid." Jones: "Well, at least Anderson and Belnap do. But that only means that modus ponens is not a tautological entailment in their technical sense. And that only means that modus ponens does not have a certain normal form. Procrustean definitions of relevance are no better than theories of types. They may eliminate some paradoxes, but they eliminate infinitely many innocent arguments too. Thus they do not even correspond with the relevant, much less explain what it is to be relevant."

The truth is that the intuition my three conversations capture is precisely the intuition that extensional truth-ground containment is a form of logical relevance. There is no denying the existence or the familiarity of this logical intuition, since millions of Venn and other diagrams capture it too.

A third and still deeper reply is that the relevantists simply do not understand the modern classical project. They do not take seriously what Quine calls the "aims and claims of regimentation" (1975/1960: ch. 5, § 33). Frege, Russell, the early

Wittgenstein, and Quine are all abundantly clear that for their project of achieving a formally adequate analysis of sciences in general and mathematics in particular, ordinary language use is *not* to be faithfully and precisely described or preserved, but *replaced*, or better, *regimented* for the limited purpose of truth preservation (see e.g. Whitehead 1978/1910: 1–3, 12). They are *not* ordinary language philosophers. If the *relevantists* wish to formalize ordinary "if" to explore ordinary language relevance, well and good, but it does not follow that modern classical logicians wish to, or should. In fact, it is disingenuous to pretend that modern classical logicians are secretly insincere or do not know exactly what they are doing when they use technical notions like material implication.

In fact, there is a problem of paraphrase with Stevenson's argument after all. Namely, while his first quoted statement is grammatically an indicative conditional, logically it is a subjunctive conditional. For it is normally taken to mean that if God *were* to exist, then there *would* be no evil. And this is why its denial is normally not taken to imply that God exists and evil does not. And that is why modern classical logicians agree with the relevantists that subjunctive conditionals fall outside modern classical logic. The only disagreement is on whether subjunctive conditionals should be studied in logic at all; and here I agree with the relevantists that they should be, to the extent possible.[3]

A fourth and elegant reply is that the relevantists overlook what Shahid Rahman calls the epistemic constraint on modern classical logic (Rahman 2001). Anderson and Belnap apparently believe that modern classical logicians would actually use the falsehood (or impossibility) of a premiss to materially (or strictly) imply the truth of a conclusion (Anderson 1975: 17–18). But I think Russell speaks for all modern classical logicians when he says:

There is also a practical ground for the neglect of such implications, for, speaking generally, they can only be *known* when it is already known either that their hypothesis is false or that their conclusion is true; and in neither of these cases do they serve to make us know the conclusion, since in the first case the conclusion need not be true, and in the second it is known already. Thus such implications do not serve the purpose for which implications are chiefly useful, namely that of making us know, by deduction, conclusions of which we were previously ignorant. (1978/1910: 20–21, Russell's emphasis)

Russell explains more fully:

The reason that proofs are used at all is that we can sometimes perceive that q **follows from** p, when we should not otherwise know that q is true; while in other cases, "p implies q" is only to be inferred either from the falsehood of p or from the truth of q. In these other cases, the proposition "p implies q" serves no practical purpose; it is only when this proposition is **used as a means of discovering** the truth of q that it is useful. Given a true proposition p, there will be some propositions q such that the truth of "p implies q" is evident, and thence the truth of q is inferred; while in the case of other true propositions [q], their truth must be independently known before we can know that p implies them. (Russell 1994a/ ca. 1903–9005: 515, my bold emphasis; see 21)

Russell calls the constraint practical. He means that we would have no practical reason to infer to an already known truth, or from an already known falsehood. This is a form of pragmatic relevance. And Rahman (2001: 100) is right that, at least as Russell discusses it, it definitely has an epistemic aspect. In any case, Quine says that ignoring the constraint is just why the odd-looking inferences look odd in the first place (Quine 1983: 17; 1975: 222); see also the very helpful Wright (1967/1957b) and Geach (1980; 1980a).

More deeply, the constraint is relational. A valid logical inference must be based on and due to a formal relationship between the premisses and conclusion. This implies it cannot be based on or due to the falsehood of a premiss considered by itself, or the truth of the conclusion considered by itself. Note that on this level, the pragmatic and epistemic aspects drop out, and I think rightly so. This is a matter of formal logic, not pragmatism or epistemology, insofar as the falsehood of a premiss or the truth of the conclusion is formally determined. There is also a formal sense in which the relational aspect rules out inference from any old tautology to any old tautology. In a formal logic, we do wish to prove tautologies as theorems, but we do not wish to consider an inference valid merely because the conclusion is a tautology, or even merely because the premisses and conclusion are all tautologies, if they are all tautologies. The inference must be a formal *relationship between* the premisses and conclusion. Russell calls it deducibility.

I myself consider it a *forward* (or at least unidirectional) constraint. That is, a proof must not only be sound (valid plus all premisses true), but just as the relevantists say, it must proceed *from* the premisses *to* the conclusion. This is a form of ordered relationship; the set of premisses and the conclusion are in effect an ordered pair. This unidirectional order entails that a proof or chain of proofs must not be circular or beg the question. That is, on the forward constraint, we cannot go forward from *A* to *B* and then from *B* back to *A*. Of course, we can still prove *B* from *A* in one logic and *A* from *B* in another. But the forward constraint is also a constraint on integrating two such logics into one. That is, a successful integration of two logics into one should not make their proofs circular. I cannot discuss circularity and begging the question in detail here. Nor can we, on the forward constraint, infer from *A* to *A*, which is going neither forward not backward but standing still. Of course, $A \supset A$ is perfectly truth-ground containment relevant; but the forward constraint is a constraint on precisely such inferences.

Eighth, Wittgenstein explains following from in terms of truth-ground containment (T 5.11, 5.12); and truth-grounds are truth-possibilities (T 5.101). But Meyer says:

> The mistake is to think that one needs some *modal* intuitions to formalize entailment. [R]*equiring* such modal intuitions is overkill. If one has a decent →, the *theoremhood*, as a matter of logic, of A → B is what is needed that A should entail B. [C. I.] Lewis introduced (in effect) the □ of modern modal logics because he did *not* have a decent →; he only had ⊃. So he tried to cook up a decent → (again, in effect) by *defining* A → B as □(A ⊃ B). But, if one *already* has a decent →, it is at best redundant to *characterize* A → B as □(A ⊃ B). It may be *worse* than redundant; why should a decent → have a □ built into it in this way? (Meyer 1985: 620; see 618–30)

One reply might be that Meyer is not proving that we can never define relevance in terms of modality, but merely saying that we should not if we can avoid it. This would be analogous to Aristotle's rule for definition by genus and difference, "A definition should not be negative where it can be affirmative," where it is admitted that "many terms...are essentially negative and...*require* negative definitions" (Copi 1978: 157). Likewise, we might then argue, extensional relevance is essentially containment of truth-possibilities, and so *requires* modal definition. But this is not what Wittgenstein is saying. He is not explaining relevance in terms of modality, nor modality in terms of relevance. He is explaining *both* truth-possibilities and following from (as containment of truth-possibilities) in terms of *truth tables*, and therefore ultimately in terms of *logical form*. And if he has a decent concept of truth tables, we would *expect* his concept of extensional following from to follow from that. Where else could it come from? In fact, showing an entailment by truth table is precisely the proof of theoremhood Meyer overlooks. This is not redundant but informative analysis. The concepts of extensional containment relevance and of necessary validity are very different, yet are logically equivalent in modern classical logic. The general concepts of a truth table and of logical form are not modal but timeless, or understood in abstraction from time; nor are they relevant, since relevance (and validity) apply only to inferences and to conditional statements.

Meyer is implicitly objecting against Wittgenstein's view that truth-possibilities define truth-ground containment, and thus define relevance in terms of modality. Indeed, truth-grounds *are* truth-possibilities. But truth-possibilities are definable in turn as combinations of truth-values, i.e., as rows on truth tables, i.e., ultimately as part of logical form. Thus truth-possibilities are truth-functional, innocent, and most importantly, eliminatively analyzed away (as is relevance). Meyer, of course, is not discussing Wittgenstein or Russell here, but C. I. Lewis.

Ninth, Nicholas Griffin objects that "the term 'relevant logic' [now has] a specific meaning" which excludes modern classical logic (Griffin 2001: 293). My reply is that insisting on established meanings to settle philosophical issues has all "the advantages of theft over honest toil" (Russell 1919: 71). It begs the question, sweeps the issues under a definitional rug, and closes the mind. Griffin is refusing to permit any new inquiry into the concept of relevance. Many other meanings were once thought to be well settled too, for example, that physical matter is corpuscular in Newton's sense. This ironically inverts Griffin, who is on the wrong side of his own comparison (2001: 293). It is Anderson and Belnap's atomic statements that equate to Newton's corpuscles. People like Griffin once refused to reclassify whales as mammals because it was well settled that the term "whale" meant 'big fish (with whale differentiae)', which excludes mammals. Closer to home, Griffin has placed himself in the position of logicians who believed logic was final and complete in Aristotle. For Griffin believes that the concept of relevance is final and complete in Anderson and Belnap. But like all science, relevance moves on.

What really matters is not which definition is given earlier or later in time, but which definition is best. We can stipulate how we use the word "relevant" or "physical" as a verbal convention, but we cannot stipulate the best answer to a philosophical or scientific question. Nor should we judge a term incorrectly used merely because it becomes broader or narrower in scope than is now the convention. Griffin rejects my view merely because it makes modern classical logic a relevance logic (2001: 293). The truth is that as our concepts improve, our classifications improve, and our terms change in meaning and scope. Indeed, as our definitions improve, synthetic sentences can even become analytic and vice versa (Russell 1976: 139, 247). Is not what we count as belonging to a species relative to our concept of that species? Would we really wish to insist that a whale is a fish merely because "fish" has a conventional meaning, 'finned animal that lives and swims in water'? Yet just as whales can be and have been reclassified as mammals on a deeper conception of what a mammal is, so too modern classical logic can be reclassified as relevant on a deeper conception of what relevance is.

Tenth and last, Millôr Fernandez says, "A picture is worth a thousand words, but try to say that in a picture" (Varadarajan 2012: 7 quoting Fernandez). My reply is that you *can* say that in a *logic diagram* in infinitely many diagram logics. And there is no a priori reason why natural languages are not diagrammatic. Indeed, some pictographic natural languages are at least somewhat diagrammatic.

7. Definitions, Theses, and Constraints for Modern Classical Logic

Logicians generally begin with definitions; philosophers generally end with them (Robinson 1950: 3–4). In any case, it seems best to me to summarize my definitions, theses, and constraints for modern classical relevance only now.

I begin with one definition of validity and two definitions of truth-ground relevance for propositional logic.

(a) An argument is (formally, deductively) *valid* =Df it is (formally) logically impossible for all the premisses to be true and the conclusion false.

The parenthetically included terms are meant to exclude cases of synthetic a priori inference, such as from an apple's being red to its having color, or to its not being green. These inferences too seem to involve relevant inclusions or exclusions in their own way, but go too far afield for us here.

(b) An argument *follows with truth table containment-relevance* =Df its truth table is such that the truth-grounds of the premisses contain the truth-grounds of the conclusion, meaning it is not the case that on any row in the table, all the premisses are true and the conclusion false. Wittgenstein's actual definition is stated twice in the *Tractatus*:

> T 5.11 If all the truth-grounds that are common to a number of propositions are at the same time truth-grounds of a certain proposition, then we say that the truth of that proposition **follows from** the truth of the others.

T 5.12 In particular, the truth of a proposition '*p*' **follows from** the truth of another proposition '*q*' if all the truth-grounds of the latter are truth-grounds of the former. (my bold emphasis)

Or as Wright puts it:

If all truth-conditions of one truth-function[al proposition] are also truth-conditions of another truth-function[al proposition], the first function is said to entail the second. (Wright 1967/1957a: 25; see 32)

This definition should be clear to anyone who understands truth tables. Namely, an argument *follows with truth table containment-relevance* =Df on any row in the argument's truth table on which the premisses are true, the conclusion is also true.

(c) An argument *follows with literally geometrical containment-relevance* =Df to draw the premisses is already to draw the conclusion in Shin's propositional diagram logic Venn-I (Shin 1994: ch. 3). Where "wfd" means well-formed diagram and "*D*" means some specific diagram, Shin's definition of the consequence relation for Venn-I is:

Wfd D follows from set of *wfds* $\triangle$ (i.e., $\triangle \vDash D$) if and only if every set assignment that satisfies every member of $\triangle$ also satisfies *D* (i.e., $\forall_s (\forall_{D_D{}^1 \in \triangle} s \vDash D^1 \triangle \rightarrow s \vDash D))$. (Shin 1994: 72)

I cannot describe Shin's semantics here, but I think the reader can see the sort of containment involved easily enough; "set assignment that satisfies" is equivalent to "truth-ground." See Shin (1994: 119) for her similar definition of the consequence relation for her quantificational diagram logic Venn-II.

Definitions (a)–(c) allow me to state three biconditional theses. (1) An argument is valid if and only if it follows with truth table containment-relevance. (2) An argument is valid if and only if it follows with literally geometrical containment-relevance. (3) An argument follows with truth table containment-relevance if and only if it follows with literally geometrical containment-relevance. Theses (1)–(3) appear to be synthetic a priori logical equivalences. And definitions (a)–(c) appear to be distinct only in reason. If I am right, then the insight that modern classical validity is visibly containment-relevant is the sort of insight that was right in front of us all the time. Philosophy often involves observing obvious things which many people overlook. And there is no reason why modern classical logicians cannot admit synthetic a priori truths. Frege does in geometry, and Russell does in indefinitely many fields. Besides, a synthetic thesis is significant in a way an analytic thesis cannot be. That is, if I am right, then theses (1)–(3) can be taken as explanations in Frege's sense of factually informative explanation. This Fregean sense of explanation applies to any pair of logically equivalent statements or expressions one of which is more illuminating than the other (Dejnožka 2003: 70; 1981: 37). In theses (1)–(2), surely the consequent illuminates and explains the antecedent. That is, surely truth-ground relevance illuminates and explains validity. But in thesis (3), I suggest that antecedent and consequent illuminate each other in different ways. For the antecedent of thesis (3) is more abstractly or intellectually visible—I would like to say literally clearer. But the consequent is more concretely visible in the sense of ordinary pictures—I would like to say easier on the eye. Thus I suggest they help explain each other. There is always room for more investigation of these issues, but that would take us too far afield here.

Since virtually all modern classical logicians from Wittgenstein on would accept at least thesis (1), virtually all are implicitly extensional relevantists.

In contrast, the following three theses are obviously incorrect for modern classical logic. (4) An argument is valid if and only if it satisfies the Anderson-Belnap variable sharing requirement. (5) An argument follows with literally geometrical containment-relevance if and only if it satisfies Anderson-Belnap variable sharing. (6), An argument follows with truth table containment-relevance if and only if it satisfies Anderson-Belnap variable sharing.

Concerning definition (b), there are at least six trivially different ways to explain truth table containment; they all apply *mutatis mutandis* to definition (c) as well. Where *P* entails *Q*: (1) *Set inclusion*. The set of truth-grounds of *P* includes the set of truth-grounds of *Q*. (2) *Set membership*. All the truth-grounds of *P* are members of the set of truth-grounds of *Q*. (3) *Universal hypothetical*. If anything is a truth-ground of *P*, then it is a truth-ground of *Q*. (4) *Truth condition set inclusion*. The set of combinations of atomic facts (or elementary states of affairs) which make *P* true includes the set of combinations of atomic facts (or elementary states of affairs) which make *Q* true. Or more simply, the set of *P* fact combinations includes the set of *Q* fact combinations. (5) *Truth condition set membership*. All the *P* fact combinations are members of the set of *Q* fact combinations. (6) *Truth condition universal hypothetical*. If anything is a *P* fact combination, then it is a *Q* fact combination. Ways (1)–(3) mirror or reflect ways (4)–(6). Ways (1)–(3) concern truth-values on truth table rows, and ways (4)–(6) concern conditions which make statements true. Ways (4)–(6) can be understood in turn in two different ways: as *truth-as-correspondence realist metaphysics* following the Tractarian Wittgenstein, (4a)–(6a), or *disquotationally* following the Tarskian Quine (4b)–(6b). For present purposes of defining extensionalist relevant containment, the differences among these nine ways of analyzing "contains," important as they may be for metaphysics (realism versus antirealism, and universals versus classes), make no difference. I mean that the same entailments, such as modus ponens, are trivially validated by all of them. More than that, I mean that anyone who accepts all of them will find them distinct only in reason. I use "truth-condition" to mean condition making a statement true, since Wittgenstein seems to use "truth-ground" for combinations of atomic truth-values making (in the very different, merely truth-functional sense of "make") a statement true. The difference is especially clear in the case of atomic statements. No atomic statement can make itself true in the sense of being its own truth-condition, as if it were an ontological argument for its own truth. But every atomic statement is its own truth-ground, since that merely means that on every row on which it is true, it is true.

But there is a further distinction which *is* important here. It is best introduced as an ambiguity in ways (3) and (6) concerning universal hypotheticals. This is the distinction between traditional "all" and modern classical "any" concerning existential import. The issue is the validity of modern classical ex contradictione. If we analyze "*P* & ¬*P*, therefore *Q*" as a case of truth-ground containment in the merely negative sense that there is no row in the truth table for the argument on which the premiss is true and the conclusion false, simply because there is no row on which the premiss is true, then we preserve ex contradictione, but appear to have departed from our positive conception of a truth-ground as a truth-possibility which makes a given statement true. In fact, if we cannot equate the double negative "there is no row on which the premiss is true and the conclusion not true" with the positive "the conclusion is true on every row on which the premiss is true," then our modern classical analysis of truth-ground containment for ex contradictione seems to abandon modern classical negation, on which all double negations vanish. But I think the best diagnosis is that the problem is due to the difference between traditional "all," which has existential import, and modern classical "any," which does not. For the problem arises only if we use "all," and vanishes if we use "any." That is, we can analyze "The truth-grounds of '*P* & ¬*P*' contain the truth-grounds of '*Q*'" as meaning, "If '*P* & ¬*P*' is true on any row, then '*Q*' is true on that row." This has no existential import, meaning it does not imply that there is any row on which "*P* & ¬*P*" is true. Thus it can be (and is) logically equivalent to the double negative "There is no row on which '*P* & ¬*P*'" is true and '*Q*' is false." It was only the existential import of non-modern classical "all" which gave rise to the problem. This may be called the per impossibile sense of modern classical relevant containment. That is, I am really saying, "If '*P* & ¬*P*' is, perhaps per impossibile, true on any row, then '*Q*' is true on that row." After all, "*P* & ¬*P*" cannot be true on any row!

One might object that this negative sense of truth-ground containment, on which we count truth as preserved just in case no row makes the premises true and the conclusion false, is not containment of truth at all. For even if using modern "if any" makes this negative sense clear and intelligible as a per impossibile sense, how can we seriously claim that truth is preserved when neither the premises nor the conclusion *are* true, nor *can* be true, as in *A* & ¬*A*, therefore *B* & ¬*B*, or even as in *A* & ¬*A*, therefore *A* & ¬*A*? Is this not a merely arbitrary "default" sense? How can an *arbitrary* sense of truth-ground containment, however bright or clear the line it draws as a precising definition, be a *relevant* sense? One reply is that the objection is irrelevant to the issue of relevance, as the relevantists portray relevance. Specifically, it commits the informal relevance fallacy of false (logical) cause (*non causa pro causa*). If you please, it is a red herring, a distractor from the main issue. For the relevantists chose to draw their own arbitrary bright line as to what relevance is. They largely chose to regard rejection of modus ponens and disjunctive syllogism as being what is essential to, even definitive of, relevance. And the negative "per impossibile" sense of truth-ground containment is simply irrelevant to evaluating *those* two argument forms, since *they* preserve truth in the *positive* sense. That is, they have rows on which their conclusions and all their premises are *true*. But this reply is a mere ad hominem. Even if on their own concept of relevance, the relevantists are inconsistent in criticizing ex contradictione as irrelevant, the objection may still have merit. Indeed, I would be the first to say there is more to relevance than the reliability of modus ponens and disjunctive syllogism. My actual reply is simply that inferring arbitrariness from precision is a non sequitur. There can be reasons for regimentation. And the negative sense was not picked out of a hat. On it, truth *does not fail to be contained*. Is that not a very good and relevant reason for considering the negative sense a very relevant sense of truth preservation? Indeed, except for positive truth containment, what could be a better sort of containment? Thus this reply, too, finds that the objection commits a fallacy of relevance, this time simpliciter or per se.

Perhaps the reasons given here for and against the negative sense of truth preservation are incommensurable, circular, or even mere semantics, and in that sense ultimately a matter of logical taste. If so, my reply may be weak; but on this level, the objection is just as weak. And I think my reply states a good reason.

Of course, all this concerns only the relevant *validity* of ex contradictione. Modern classical relevant *soundness* is violated because the premiss cannot be true. What Rahman calls the epistemic constraint is violated as well. That is perhaps the best reply of all. And this brings us to our next topic.

There are at least five basic relevance filters or constraints which modern classical logicians can use and remain modern classical logicians. Or if you please, there is the genus of truth-ground relevant containment, plus at least five modern classical species of relevance, before we even come to consider relevantist species (or sub-species).

First, there is the compossibility constraint that it be logically possible that all the premisses be true. In truth tables, this is the constraint that there be at least one row in which all the premisses are true. This eliminates ex contradictione quodlibet.

Second, there is the soundness constraint that all the premisses be true. In truth tables, this is the constraint that there be at least one row in which all the premisses are true of the actual world. This constraint eliminates ex falso sequitur. The soundness constraint entails (includes) the compossibility constraint, since the existence of a row in which all the premisses are true of the actual world entails (includes) the existence of a row in which all the premisses are true of *some* possible world. Anderson and Belnap miss this when they ridicule modus ponens (material implication) via "counterexamples" using false minor premisses (false antecedents) which they rightly say no one would seriously make. No one makes them because of the soundness constraint. The soundness constraint eliminates the paradoxes of ex falso (a false statement implies every statement), and of course also the paradoxes of ex contradictione / ex impossibile (a contradictory / impossible statement implies every statement).

Modern classical logic texts generally permit starting from false or impossible premisses only in the sense of assumptions made and then refuted in indirect argument, i.e., reductio ad absurdum. This is so, for example, in Copi (proving assumptions false) and Jeffrey (falsifiability trees). This goes to the fact that the one thing material implication disallows is going from a truth to a falsehood. For if an assumption implies a contradiction or other absurdity, the modern classical logician then in virtue of that very fact rejects the assumption as false (or at least untrue), because it cannot be true. This is the basis of Jeffrey's falsifiability tree method for modern classical logic. Jeffrey proves validity by assuming the conclusion to be false and then showing that every branch of truth-flow leads to a contradiction. In effect, he is using indirect argument as a meta-argument to show the validity of the given argument. I shall return to indirect argument shortly.

Third, there is the (negative) epistemic (Rahman), practical (Russell), or forward (Dejnožka) constraint. That is, the validity of an inference must be determined in some way *other than* by merely resting content with being already given the truth of the conclusion and/or the untruth (not necessarily falsehood) of some premiss. This eliminates both paradoxes of material implication: denial of the antecedent (ex falso) (a false statement implies every statement); and affirmation of the consequent (any statement implies every true statement).[1] It also eliminates both paradoxes of strict implication: an impossible statement implies every statement; and any statement implies every necessary statement. This constraint is not wholly negative. "Forward" does have some positive content. It indicates not only that we are not to rest content with the conclusion's truth and/or some premiss's nontruth as already given, but that we are to go in a forward direction from premisses to conclusion (except in indirect argument). This is good. We want more than a cooked stipulation that we are simply doing away with the paradoxes of material implication. But the constraint is only minimally positive. It utterly fails to specify *how* to go forward. It does not say to use formal deductive means as opposed to a priori intuition, or even as opposed to inductive means. Insofar as we can successfully go forward to prove something only if all the premisses are true, the forward constraint entails (includes) the soundness constraint. Note that there is nothing epistemic or practical in the mere concept of going in a forward direction as such.

The forward constraint might be better named the directional constraint, or even better, the unidirectional constraint. For we go in a backward direction in indirect proof, at least relative to what we want to show. Namely, we try to prove that a conclusion follows by proving that the untruth of at least one premiss follows from the denial of the conclusion. Of course, the actual work of proof is still going forward, only now we are starting from the denial of the conclusion, and seeking to arrive at the untruth of at least one premiss. Thus the forward constraint is still well named for the actual work of proof. But then we flip it around because we really aim to show validity going forward from the premisses to the conclusion in the original argument. It is only relative to this aim that indirect proof goes in a backward direction. Therefore I will keep the terminology of forward constraint, with the proviso that in a relative sense indirect proof goes backward.

Does the forward constraint rule out *A*, therefore *A*? Looking to what *A* says, we are not really going forward from one thing to another, but resting in place with the same thing. Looking to syntax, we are not going forward in the formal sense that premiss and conclusion are formally identical. We are going forward only in the formal sense of sign-tokens as opposed to sign-types. And this second formal sense is a merely nominal sense of going forward. This must not be confused with the fact that *A*, therefore *A* is truth-ground containment relevant, hence extensionally valid. That is precisely what the constraint functions to constrain here. Nor must it be confused with the issues of circularity or of begging the question, which are issues of fallacy (which also must not be confused with each other). We can still allow the inference *A*, therefore *A* if we wish, but we should be clear that we cannot consistently also adopt the forward constraint, except in the nominal sense described. A fallacy is a way an argument can *go wrong*, not necessarily a way an argument can *be invalid*. Even valid arguments can be useless for purposes of proof. *Mere* validity, I want to say, is no guarantee of argumentative interest or value.

One might object that using the truth table method does not involve going forward, but so to speak takes in the whole truth table at once, at least from the logical point of view. I shall postpone my reply until I discuss Wittgenstein at the end of this chapter.

Fourth, there is the (positive) deducibility constraint that the (formal) validity of an inference be showable *by some formal means*. That is, it must be showable that the premisses and conclusion are logically (formally) related or connected. This may also be called the formal validity constraint. That is, the conclusion must be formally deducible from the premisses. This rules out synthetic a priori intuition and induction. It is hard for me to believe anyone would seriously think that modern classical logicians would not impose this constraint. Russell, for one, is express on the point. He distinguishes among material implication, formal implication, and deductively valid inference as early as 1903 in *The Principles of Mathematics*. He says that mathematics "consists of deduction" (Russell 1964/1938: 4). He says that "all mathematics is deduction by logical principles from logical principles" (Russell 1964/1938: 5). He says, "By the help of ten principles of deduction and ten other principles of a general logical nature..., all mathematics can be strictly and formally deduced" (Russell 1964/1938: 4). He speaks of deduction in *Principia*, narrowing his earlier *Principles* list of ten deductive principles down to five; years later he narrows the list down to one deductive principle due to Nicod and using the Sheffer stroke. In his 1914 *Our Knowledge of the External World*, he says that premiss and conclusion in deductive inference must be *connected*; the conclusion must *follow from* the premisses (Russell 1960/1929: 49–50). Deducibility is a *whole-part relation* (Russell 1960/1929: 63). In *Introduction to Mathematical Philosophy*, he speaks of "formal deducibility" (Russell 1919: 153), and distinguishes it from formal implication (accidental generalization, equivalent to a class of material implications) every time he discusses it (Russell 1919: 145–46, 149, 152–53).

Meyer says that if relevance:

means anything in logic, it means that we want what the premisses of a valid argument state to be *related* to what its conclusion states; and we at least wish to avoid arguments whose premisses follow from *totally unrelated* premisses. A decent implication is *essentially relational*" And I must observe again that modern [classical] logic...has abandoned this insistence when it comes to the fundamental logical relation of entailment. Here an *accidental* conjunction of truths will do (if one thinks of *materially sound* arguments); if one wants one's arguments to be *formally sound* (in a sense attributable to Russell, which, despite claims that he was "confused," has dominated the subject ever since), all that one requires moreover is that the accident be universal. (As in the phrase, "*Whenever* the premisses are true, the conclusion is also true.") (Meyer 1985: 609, his emphasis)

Thus Meyer knows Russell no better than Anderson and Belnap do. He correctly distinguishes Russell's relation of material implication from Russell's relation of formal implication, and correctly notes that both are accidental. He even correctly notes that the difference is that, so to speak, material implication is a particular implication while formal implication is a universal implication, or in effect a class of material implications (Russell 1964/1938: 13). But he misses Russell's relation of deducibility altogether, as well as Russell's endorsement of Wittgenstein's view that deducibility is containment of truth-grounds. This is not to mention missing Wittgenstein. Ironically, Meyer is in closer agreement with Wittgenstein's and Russell's concept of relevance than he thinks. For deducibility as containment of truth-grounds is precisely an *essential relationship*, not an accidental one. Thus Meyer misses the one relationship of importance, or if you please, the relationship of greatest relevance, to the issue of relevance in Russell and Wittgenstein.

The deducibility constraint entails (includes) the forward constraint. At least it does if we add soundness, making it the *sound deducibility* constraint. (I am still postponing the objection that truth tables do not go in a forward direction but are viewed as a whole; truth tables are a deductive method.) Note that there is nothing epistemic or practical in the mere concept of formal deducibility as such.

Fifth, there is the indexing constraint that every premiss be both true and formally used in the formal validity proof. As I very carefully worded the constraint, it entails (includes) the deducibility constraint. This constraint may also be called the relevant use constraint. We may, if we wish, weaken it to include premisses that *can* be used to arrive at the conclusion, but need not actually be, following Anderson and Belnap (1975: 31). The difference makes no difference for our main purposes here.

In simplest terms, to index is to assign a number to each premiss, so we can tell whether and where each premiss is used in a proof. For example, in modus ponens we number the premisses 1 and 2 and number the conclusion 3, and write "1, 2" as our justification (usually to the right) of the conclusion. That is, at each stage in the proof, we cite any premisses we use by number. Note that this entails (includes) our being able to count *how often* each premiss is used (compare Meyer (1985: 616; see 617). We can also number our rules of inference if we have any, and even number the number of times we use each rule, preferably with a different set of number-expressions for the sake of clarity.

The indexing constraint may also be called the *fully* forward-looking constraint. Of course, the sound deducibility constraint is already forward-looking (we deduce something from something), and the forward constraint obviously is as well. But the indexing constraint is fully forward-looking in the following sense. The index numbers for the premisses that justify our arriving at a given statement are always lower than the index number of the given statement itself. And the conclusion always has the highest number, and its number can never appear in the justification for any premiss. (This is as opposed to the index number for an assumption which is the *denial* of the conclusion in an indirect proof.) Thus indexing is visibly forward-looking every step of the way. Indeed, is the justificational indexing to the right of each premiss not itself a sort of chart, table, or diagram of relevant use? Certainly it can at least complete the labeling of what is going on in a logic diagram, so as to help us go through the diagram in an orderly way, if our limited ability prevents our directly seeing that the conclusion follows. This last purpose is merely practical, insofar as a well-formed diagram should already be orderly.

Indexing is a common practice among modern classical logicians. Most learn some form of it in their first logic course. Frege uses a form of indexing in *Begriffsschrift*, and also in *Grundgesetze*. Whitehead and Russell use indexing in *Principia*. Quine uses indexing much like that of *Principia* in his logic books. I cannot discuss the forms of indexing in any detail here. Nor am I concerned to trace the earlier history of indexing in logic and mathematics. To mention just a single strand, Sylvan says "Ticket entailment in general...has a long history" (Sylvan 2000: 135 n.87); ticket entailment is "an even stricter form of entailment" than E, (Anderson 1975: 6). I would note only that categorical syllogisms are virtually indexed by the fact that the major premiss is always first and the minor premiss always second, and that Aristotle antedates Euclid, who does not number the steps of his proofs, but does cite his reasons as he goes along, which allows him to be indexed quite well by modern editors. My point at the moment is simply that Anderson and Belnap write as if there is no modern classical indexing at all.

There are at least five basic reasons for indexing. First and most basically, we use it to number and thereby identify and distinguish our premisses. This is most helpful for beginning arguers. Second, we use it to check elegance or economy in the sense of how long the proof is, how many steps it takes. This second use, too, concerns indexing only in the sense of numbering each step; we have not yet come to justificational use. Actually, we need not always number the steps of proofs in order to be able to see that one proof is longer than another. But it is still a reason why indexing *can* be used, so as to be exact about the counts, for example if we are comparing long handwritten proofs. Third, we can use indexing justificationally, that is, to check how the proof was done—which earlier statements were used to justify which later statements. Fourth, we can use it to check elegance or economy (relevant use) in the sense of whether there are any premisses that are not used at all. Fifth, we can check elegance or economy (relevant use) in the sense of how often each premiss is used. There can be far more sophisticated indexing, for indefinitely many more sophisticated reasons, as well. But my point is that modern classical logicians can, and I think often do, index for all, many, or some of the five basic reasons just stated, and without changing modern classical logic into a relevantist logic. For modus ponens and disjunctive syllogism are completely unaffected by indexing for any or all of these five basic reasons. For in each of these two argument-forms, there are two premisses, each premiss is necessary, and each premiss is used only once, just as in a categorical syllogism; the long premiss is the major one, and the short one the minor. Anderson-Belnap variable sharing is necessary only to Anderson-Belnap indexing, and not to modern classical indexing, nor to Aristotelian syllogistic indexing.

There is something empty about indexing for relevantists and modern classical logicians alike. It is mere accounting, and it presupposes that all the logically substantive features of proof, if I may call them that, are in place. But it completes our account of relevance, and makes all the steps visible.

Surveying this list of modern classical relevance constraints, is it not interesting that modern classical logicians not only knew of the problems but resolved them within the framework of modern classical logic, and went on to their great works of formal analyses of mathematics, science, and metaphysics? Then the relevantists came along, basically acted as if they were the first to notice the true seriousness of these problems, found them fatal to modern classical logic, and wrote off modern classical logic as a joke. The misunderstanding is so great that Anderson and Belnap say the fact that modern classical logicians "never actually argue" ex impossibile or ex falso, nor to a conclusion already known to be true, shows that they are stupid, insincere, or unserious (Anderson 1975: 5, 17–18, 328–30). But I take the same fact as showing instead that modern classical logicians either expressly or implicitly apply the modern classical relevance constraints I described. At the very least, this is a question of proper interpretation of what validity really is for modern classical logicians. Does anyone really wish to say that modern classical logicians do not wish to argue soundly, and do not wish to proceed from true premisses to a true conclusion, when they are arguing seriously or scientifically, to use the lexicon of Frege? I think charity was neither given to the modern classical logicians nor needed by them.

If these five constraints are not relevance filters, what are they? What should we call them? Yet they are all used by modern classical logicians, I would imagine most by most, if not all by all.

Sylvan's general concern with modern classical logic's misplacing relevance into the realm of epistemology (Sylvan 2000: 47-49) emerges as itself somewhat misplaced. For the so-called epistemic constraint is just one of five. It is not the most basic, nor the most complete. It is not even considered epistemic by Russell, but practical, though he uses some epistemic language. I consider it neither epistemic nor practical, but forward. And what is wrong with it? Considered in itself, that is, aside from whether its locus is epistemology, should not relevantists be applauding it?

It might be objected that it is interesting here that we can know both that P and that if P then Q, and can come to know that Q on this basis; and we can know both that P or Q and that $\neg P$, and can come to know that Q on that basis; but we cannot come to know Q on the basis of our knowing that P and $\neg P$, since we cannot know that P and $\neg P$. For we can know (to be true) only what can be true, and a contradiction cannot be true. And this suggests that modern classical logic can be implicitly glossed as an epistemic logic, with the epistemic constraint as central. Of course, I cannot explore all the details of this suggestion here. But the particular point made, even though it is expressed epistemically, properly falls under the first constraint, the compossibility constraint. For P and $\neg P$, therefore Q is already ruled out by that constraint. It is also ruled out by the soundness constraint and by the forward constraint. And not one of these three constraints is epistemic.

All this beards the relevant Lion in its den. For modus ponens and disjunctive syllogism meet all five modern classical constraints, if all their premisses are true. I find this intuitively satisfying. They are such simple argument forms, you can see their validity right through them, so to speak. And they are useful because they preserve truth in some very common, ordinary, and natural (not to say paradigmatic) reasoning situations. In fact, modus ponens is basically the *only* rule of inference in Frege's *Begriffsschrift*. (Greaves 2002: 181; Bynum 1972: 61; Heijenoort 1967a: 2, 4; see Frege 1977/1879: 7–8, "The restriction...to a single mode of inference"). Thus relevantists must basically find no valid arguments in *Begriffsschrift* at all, despite its many great achievements (Bynum 1972: 13–14; Heijenoort 1967a: 2–5), and its arguably being "the first major advance in logic since Aristotle" (Bynum 1972: 12), and even "perhaps the most important single work ever written in logic" (Heijenoort 1967a: 1). Granted, most great works must be strictly false, insofar as they say opposing things; but as an objection here, I think this is stretching it. Indeed, as Bynum says, "Frege's major rule of inference—a rule of detachment (*modus ponens*)...fits very nicely with his desire to minimize the possibility of mistakes" (Bynum 1972: 61, his emphasis).

I think it is this very transparency that makes it so easy to think that modern classical logic banishes or has no place for intensionality. That is, of course, a big mistake, historically as well as conceptually. Frege distinguishes sense from reference. Whitehead and Russell distinguish at least four senses of "intension" and "extension" in *Principia* (see page 111). Russell says that in *Principia*, he "thought of relations...almost exclusively as *intensions*" (Russell 1985/1959: 67, Russell's emphasis). He says "it is the intension alone which gives unity to the set,....unity to a class," and order to an ordered couple (Russell 1985/1959: 67). He says that in *Principia*, "propositional functions...are constituted by intension except as regards the variable or variables" (Russell 1985/1959: 92). Mainstream modern classical logic has both intension and extension on each of its five levels of relevant filtering. Even its extensional conception of relevance as truth-ground containment can only be intensionally *described*. This obvious fact, too, is invisible to the relevantists.

How would the early Wittgenstein, the chief and most deeply intuitive relevantist of modern classical logic, regard our list of constraints?

I think Wittgenstein would accept the compossibility and soundness constraints. His insistence that everything (or more deeply nothing) follows from a contradiction and that a tautology follows from everything (or more deeply from nothing) concerns only their validity as extreme poles of the logical structure of inference (T 4.46–4.4661; 5.142–5.143). With the exception of mutual entailment, where P and Q "are one and the same proposition" (T 5.141; compare Wright 1967/1957a: 25), a valid conclusion always "says...less" than the premisses say (T 5.14). Thus truth-ground entailment is, with the exception of mutual entailment, always containment of a logically proper sub-part. It takes scarcely any charity to suppose he would never actually argue from contradictory premisses, nor even from false premisses, but would insist that proofs have only true premisses. I doubt anyone has ever said otherwise.

Thus I agree with Richard M. McDonough that Wittgenstein "anticipates" the relevantists even while remaining a modern classical logician (McDonough 1986: 89; 264–65 n.5). McDonough speaks of ex falso (McDonough 1986: 264 n.5), but his argument is really about ex contradictione (or ex impossibile) quodlibet:

> Wittgenstein is making a point about the nature, not challenging the existence, of the "proof."....[H]e is only saying that this "proof" must be conceived differently from the proof of a genuine proposition by means of logic.
>
> Strictly speaking, nothing is proved in the "proof" that anything follows from a contradiction....One has only, in a mechanical manipulation of signs, shown that '(P & not-P) ⊃ Q' is a tautology. (McDonough 1986: 93)

That is, there are two levels to interpreting Wittgenstein here. On the shallower level, he would agree that P & $\neg P$, therefore Q, is valid for any old Q, and in this sense would admit that a contradiction entails anything and everything. But on the deeper level, he would say that a contradiction entails nothing whatsoever, since (P & $\neg P$) ⊃ Q is a mere play of symbols, an empty tautology that says nothing about the world. That is, in tautologies and contradictions alike, the logical symbols are not playing the role they play in logically contingent statements. They are not functioning to help formulate contingent statements about the world, but are emptily interacting only with each other. Thus on the deeper level, ex contradictione nihil sequitur (nothing follows from a contradiction) precisely because a contradiction is nothing, and de nihilo nihil fit (nothing follows from nothing). McDonough has an excellent and extensive scholarly argument for this which I cannot describe here (McDonough 1986: ch. 2–4; see especially ch. 3; see also Landini 2007: ch. 4).

This also explains why Wittgenstein disallows inference from the contingent to the necessary, and from the impossible to the contingent. That is because for Wittgenstein, propositions divide into the logical (empty, formal) and the contingent (genuinely about the world). For him, proof in logic is different from using logic to infer things about the world. The latter must have a contingent conclusion *and* include at least one contingent premiss. Thus inference from an impossibility or to a necessary truth is a mere empty proof in logic, and is not about the world. This is, of course, consistent with his accepting the forward constraint on the deeper level, since that constraint rules out just such inferences.

Gregory Landini adds:

Wittgenstein writes that "tautologies and contradictions show that they say nothing"; they "lack sense" but are "part of the symbolism" (TLP 4.461). Venn's propositional diagrams nicely illustrate Wittgenstein's ideas. In a logically perfect language the status of an expression as tautologous, contradictory, or contingent is built into (shown by) the syntactic conditions for the representation of genuine assertions. A propositional tautology shades nothing, and contingencies shade some but not all areas. In Venn diagrams, tautologies and contradictions are not genuine statements. A genuine statement is made by shading some, but not all, areas of the diagram. All tautologies have nothing shaded; they are just the overlapping circles—the scaffolding. [And all contradictions shade everything. "P & $\neg P$" shades the P-area and also all not-P areas.] Indeed, in Venn's propositional diagrams, [all] formulas that are logically equivalent have exactly one and the same representation. (Landini 2007: 123; see ch. 4 generally)

This beautifully ties modern classical logic in general, and the early Wittgenstein in particular, with literally geometrical diagrams. Landini shows that and how everything follows from a contradiction, and that and how a tautology follows from everything, with visible representation of the truth-ground containments in Venn propositional diagrams.

I think Wittgenstein would accept the forward constraint at least implicitly. He may not seem to be forward-looking, since he rejects rules of inference as "superfluous" (T 5.132, 6.126–6.1271), and simply inspects truth tables to check the validity of inferences (T 5.132, 6.1262). He says "process and result are equivalent" (T 6.1261), and "[p]roof...is merely a mechanical expedient to facilitate the recognition of tautologies" (T 6.1262). Yet surely he *logically* must construct truth tables correctly before he can inspect them, so as to know he is inspecting the key premiss and conclusion rows correctly. And even if he uses no rules of inference, there is forward direction in the very fact that a conclusion follows from the premisses. To eliminate rules of inference is not to eliminate following from. He says, "If p follows from q, I can make an inference from q to p, deduce p from q." (T 5.132). And this is the decisive point. Truth tables are a method of deducibility, and deducibility is always forward-looking. We always deduce something from something. Obviously, the whole point of using truth tables to check validity is to see if the conclusion follows from the premisses!

Wittgenstein clearly accepts the deducibility constraint. "If p follows from q, I can make an inference from q to p, deduce p from q" (T 5.132). Following from, or truth-ground containment, is an "internal relation" between premisses and conclusion (T 5.13–5.132; see 5.2–5.2341). That is, if the relation ceases to obtain, then the relata cannot remain the same.

Paradoxically, though Wittgenstein does not use indexing in the *Tractatus*, and simply looks to the truth table to confirm the validity of any given argument, the book itself—its entire development as a argument for his philosophy—is in effect indexed in great detail by the section numbers. I see this as deeply connected to the paradox that Wittgenstein rejects his own philosophy as unsayable at the end of the book. For if it were sayable, then on his own view he should be able to confirm it by means of a gigantic truth table, and not need to write a linear book at all. More deeply, the very concept of a truth table implies a fixed order of rows and columns. In a truth table, there is a place for everything and everything is in its place. Thus all rows can be assigned index numbers. And all the rows play an essential role in confirming a valid inference. For the procedure demands that they all be checked in order to show validity. Every row must be checked, and need be checked only once. Of course, to show *invalidity*, we can stop as soon as we find a row on which all the premisses are true and the conclusion false. And of course, if we *reject* the constraints, we can stop if we find a premiss column where the premiss is always false, or find that the conclusion column is always true, in order to show validity.

After discussing inference, Wittgenstein immediately goes on to accept disjunctive syllogism (T 5.1311). That might be accidental relative to the later relevantist critique, but with a little charity it is prescient. He says that the form of disjunctive syllogism "is masked" by the usual system, but when it is rewritten in a certain way using the Sheffer stroke, "then the inner connexion becomes obvious" (T 5.1311). But how does that make the inner connection obvious? Black's "best conjecture" is Wittgenstein thinks that somehow the Sheffer stroke makes it clear (Black 1970: 242). I think it is the *containment of truth-grounds* in the truth table that not only makes the inner connection clear, but constitutes it. Perhaps then Wittgenstein thinks the Sheffer stroke (or perhaps the Sheffer dagger) reflects this containment better than disjunction and negation, or at least simplifies our logical lexicon (compare Black 1970: 242; Quine 1986: 8; Landini 2007: 108–10).

Later on, Wittgenstein accepts modus ponens. In fact, he says, "Every proposition of logic is a *modus ponens* represented in signs" (T 6.1264). This recalls Frege's *Begriffsschrift*, which basically uses only modus ponens.

Wittgenstein "has no patience with 'self-evidence' or 'intuition' (T 5.1363, 5.4731; see also 6.1271...)" (Black 1970: 322), and criticizes Russell (T 5.4731) and Frege (T 6.1271) on this ground. Of course, they were trying to eliminate intuition from logic too. And there seems to be no *epistemic* constraint in the *Tractatus*. But even Wittgenstein appeals to self-evidence at times, if not in inference, then at least in identifying categories of relations (T 5.42).

Wittgenstein uses not just truth tables, but also bracket diagrams, to show validity (T 6.1203). This is "a graphical way of tracing out the assignments of truth-values," and is "substantially the same as the more familiar construction and evaluation of truth-tables" (Black 1970: 323). They are really a form of truth trees.

I believe it is obvious that Wittgenstein's logical theory of probability implicitly extends his conception of extensional truth-ground containment to inductive logic (T 4.464, 5.15–5.156). Here, instead of the conclusion's being true on every row on which all the premisses are true, the conclusion is true only on a proper subset, number, or percentage of the rows on which all the premisses are true. This may be called partial or percentage truth-ground containment. For example, $P \supset Q$ has a logical probability of 75%, since it is true on three of the four rows of its truth table. This is a modern classical link between deductive and inductive logical relevance very different from the ancient link I found in Aristotle's conception of induction as a kind of intellection (Dejnožka 1999: 186). For the ancient link involves intellectual intuition, while the modern classical link is purely extensional. This is also Wittgenstein's retort to those who ridicule modern classical logicians for saying that material implication as such is a form of entailment. For modern classical logicians do *not* say that. Wittgenstein would assign material implication (not: *true* material implication) a purely logical probability of only 75%! It is only under the *truth constraint* that a material implication statement be *true* that its consequent must be true if its antecedent is true. That is not material implication as such, but as constrained by a filter. Likewise for formal implication, which may be understood as a class of material implications.

This modern concept of partial pure extensional containment may also serve as a genus of which various intensional theories of inductive relevance are species. Of course, we would expect the intensional constraints or filters in inductive logic to be very unlike the ones in deductive logic. For we must allow that one constraint on a certain purely logical probability might give it a greater probability, while another might give it a lesser probability. For example, suppose a boxing match between a good boxer and a poor one. "The good boxer will win" and "The poor boxer will win" have the same purely logical probability of 50%. But this only means that each statement can be either true or false. Clearly, the good boxer, as such, is more likely to win. For the constraint of practical likelihood makes the first statement more likely and the second statement less likely. Also, indefinitely many constraints will concern the epistemic context, which can change. So we have to be far more careful here if we try to set up a classificatory scheme of genus, species, sub-species, and so on. But the deepest point for intensional relevance is that inductive evidence can be conceived or understood in different ways. For this makes inductive evidence intensional. This includes how we conceive or understand the epistemic context, not to mention good boxers and poor boxers.

Species of inductive evidence would include theories of analogical argument and of inference to the best explanation, and any interpretation of the probability calculus, such as Aristotle's frequency theory, Keynes' logical theory, or Ramsey's subjective theory. I myself advocate a mixed theory of probability (Dejnožka 1999: 209 n.4), which for present purposes is a two species or amphibian theory.

The main classificatory point is that on the deepest level of truth-ground containment relevance, deductive logic emerges as a limiting case of inductive logic. Deductive validity is full truth-ground containment; pure extensional probability is partial truth-ground containment. And it is just as visible in the truth table. There is also an equivalent in the tree method, where only a certain limited number of branches close. Similarly for literally geometrical diagrams, where we can count the number of *areas or parts* of the diagram of the premisses which include a diagram of the conclusion. All this supports the thesis of the universality of logic (the thesis that at bottom, all logic is in some sense the same) by making deductive logic a limiting case of inductive logic at the deepest level, where tautological statements are 100% probable, contradictions are 0% probable, and all other statements (including inferential statements) are somewhere in between, in the purely extensional sense of truth-ground containment relevance. This must not be confused with the ordinary sense in which we say any true statement is 100% probable. For example, we say the probability of rain is 100% when it is raining. That is fine, but it is not purely logical probability in Wittgenstein's sense. In Wittgenstein's sense, the probability of rain is only 50% even when it is raining. Probabilities in the ordinary sense can change, but probabilities in Wittgenstein's purely logical sense cannot.

I cannot discuss Wittgenstein on relevance further here.

Every one of the five constraints blocks the ex contradictione disjunct that Anderson and Belnap reject in the normal forms of modus ponens, disjunctive syllogism, and hypothetical syllogism (pages 4–5). That was the only problem they found, so this answers their critique. Truth can flow through the other disjuncts.

One might object that constraints are like epicycles. My reply is that the analogy limps. The heliocentric and terracentric theories are empirically equivalent. But modern classical logic and relevantist logic are not theorem-equivalent at all.

8. Conclusion

Are the relevantists only half right when they accuse modern classical logic of ignoring relevance? Are there two different main kinds of logic in the mansion of deductive relevance? The quick answer is that modus ponens and disjunctive syllogisms fail the Anderson-Belnap test of tautological entailment, but the truth-grounds of their conclusions are contained in the truth-grounds of their premisses. Even in $P \& \neg P$, therefore Q, where the sole premiss does not contain the sole *atom* in the conclusion, the *truth-grounds* of the conclusion are contained in the truth-grounds of the premiss in the "any" or per impossibile sense, which is the sense relevant for truth preservation. A better answer is that indexing is done in many ways, some of which are modern classical and some of which are not. But the best answer is that condition (1), purely extensional truth-ground containment relevance, is the only condition required of all deductive logical inference. If we add any condition (2), then we are defining a species of deductive inference by adding a difference. This includes any kind of filter or constraint, including any kind of variable sharing. Mere truth-ground containment as such requires no variable sharing at all, except in the trivial sense that it requires whatever variable sharing is present in the various forms of inference that preserve truth.

Who is most deeply following the relevance tradition? Is it not Russell, who endorses the whole-part containment theory of deductive validity, who endorses Wittgenstein on containment of truth-grounds as diagrammed by truth tables, and whose logic can be diagrammed in infinitely many ways so as to show relevant containment?

Who is most deeply departing from the relevance tradition? Is it not Anderson and Belnap, who I suspect would rather reject the traditional diagram test of entailment than admit Russell as a relevantist? Is it not they who proclaim the ideology of relevance as containment, yet would reject the ontology when it comes to traditional geometrical diagrams of premisses visibly containing conclusions?

It is no good for Anderson and Belnap to say now, "We knew about modern classical deducibility as truth-ground containment all along, but we felt it beneath mentioning." They make it so clear that Russell is their chief nemesis *because* he has no concept of relevant containment validity, and yet it is so clear that Russell *does* have just such a concept, and can define tautological entailment as any deducible inference rewritable as an if-then statement that is tautological in Wittgenstein's sense of "tautology," that they are caught red-handed as logicians and as scholars. If they did read Wittgenstein and Russell on point, they did not grasp the significance of it. At least, I see no cites on point in their work.

But I cannot simply conclude that there are none so blind as those who do not wish to see. For I see both sides as equally at fault, insofar as both sides think modern classical logic banishes relevance from logic. Quine seems just as unaware of the truth-ground containment relevance of his own logic as Anderson and Belnap are, except for my quotation of him on page 34. Why would Quine not *wish* to see that? It would have been the perfect answer to the relevantists' critique of him. Therefore I think it best to conclude that everyone simply missed the point.

Russell does endorse Wittgenstein on following from. But even Russell initially disliked Wittgenstein's conception of tautology. Ronald W. Clark says:

> Wittgenstein's reduction of the problems of philosophy to semantics also meant the reduction of mathematics to tautologies, since every mathematical proof was merely a tautological transformation of what was contained in its premisses. Or as Russell put it thirty years later, "All mathematical proof consists merely in saying in other

words part or the whole of what is said in the premisses."

Neither of these two conclusions was agreeable to Russell. "I found Wittgenstein's 'Tractatus' very earnest and this implied a genuine philosophical outlook in its author," he was to write. "I did not appreciate that his work implied a linguistic philosophy. When I did we parted company....I felt a violent repulsion to the suggestion that 'all mathematics is tautology'. I came to believe this but I did not like it. I thought that mathematics was a splendid edifice, but this shows that it was built on sand." (Clark 1976: 370 quoting Russell 1973/1950: 304–; 1968)

Here I think Russell and Clark (if not Wittgenstein) wrongly conceive of the key point as essentially linguistic. On their view, one might indeed argue that which statements are tautologies depends on one's language, and that therefore logical truth is "built on sand." But the concept of truth-ground containment is not linguistic in the sense of depending on what language one uses. Quite the opposite. It is about parsing one's particular language into truth-functional logic *as opposed to* the particular language one uses. Compare the Aristotelian-medieval "mental language" theory that there is mental thinking which is universal to all humans, and which is prior to, and therefore belongs to, no one spoken or written language. Or compare Frege's more recent theory that truth-functional inferences in different languages can express the same objective, timeless, nonmental thoughts. One need not accept Aristotle's or Frege's specific theories in order to see the general point that truth-ground validity is neither language-relative nor built on sand. Of course, the historical point remains that Russell was initially reluctant to accept Wittgenstein's theory of tautology, and thereby Wittgenstein's concept of relevant containment, regardless of whether Russell's reasons were good or bad. But the historical point also remains that Russell did come to accept the theory.

I have argued that if Anderson and Belnap reject the diagram test of containment, then they reject the best and deepest concept of relevance. If I am right, then the tradition they revere implicitly equates deductive validity with truth-ground containment on the deepest level. But if they are right, then the entire Western tradition is basically non-relevant from Aristotle to Wittgenstein. For Aristotelian syllogistic, propositional logic, Venn diagrams, truth tables, and truth trees are all mutually rewritable. Nonetheless, Anderson and Belnap deserve credit for doing so much to establish their own sort of intensional relevance as a new formal field. And to be fair, even they do not seem to think their theory of tautological entailment tells, or can tell, the whole story (Anderson 1975: xxii).

What is logical relevance? I agree with Diaz that Anderson and Belnap fail to state a positive theory of what relevance is, in terms of which we can tell whether their systems capture relevant entailments, and merely offer a logic which avoids the paradoxes they dislike, and otherwise does not offend their own intuitions (Diaz 1981: 8; Diaz's book argues for this in detail). Thus they are really not theorists but just logicians. Diaz notes that this criticism, that Anderson and Belnap never say what relevance is, was made by their earliest reviewers (Diaz: 1981: 9). Anderson and Belnap basically admit as much themselves, and present their declining to offer a theory of relevance as a virtue of nuts and bolts humility (Anderson 1975: xxii).

In contrast, Wittgenstein positively and specifically states what truth-ground relevance is. Namely, a conclusion follows from its premisses if and only if the truth-grounds of the premisses contain the truth-grounds of the conclusion. And it seems that Wittgenstein's theory best satisfies our deepest intuitions of logical relevance. This is ironic because the current relevance logics, which are supposedly so different from modern classical logic merely by having a relevantist character at all, in fact differ by having a shallower, less relevant conception of relevance. A deeper irony is that they are typically based on semantic tableaux or similar semantics such as possible worlds. For there is no more basic form of such semantics than the truth tables for modern classical logic.

Sextus Empiricus argued in ancient times that all deductively valid syllogisms are circular across the board. To generalize his view in my own way, it is inherent in the very definition of deductive validity (that it is logically impossible for the conclusion to be false and all the premisses true) that the truth of the premisses already presupposes or implies, and in that sense contains, the truth of the conclusion. Indeed, that implication is just what valid inference *is*. Thus there is no more difference between deductive validity and truth-ground containment than there is between the road from Athens to Thebes and the road from Thebes to Athens, which Aristotle says differ only in formula (*Physics* 202*b*).

And this allows a second formulation of my main argument: 1. If the premisses of an argument contain its conclusion, then the argument is relevantly valid. 2. If in the very fact of deductive validity the premisses of an argument already presuppose or imply its conclusion, then the premisses contain the conclusion. 3. All deductively valid arguments presuppose or imply their conclusions. 4. Therefore modern classical logic's deductively valid arguments are relevantly valid. In fact, this appears to be a deeper argument, since it applies to linguistic logics and diagram logics alike, and to all possible logics. Even relevantists aim in effect at showing that all valid arguments are circular in their own sense or senses of "contain." Whether all valid arguments are therefore *fallacious*, or whether only some proper subset of them are appropriately deemed *fallaciously* circular, is an ancient question.[1]

What contains what in relevant entailment? Anderson and Belnap think the relata of the relevance relation are or ought to be statement intensions. But my view is that the real relata of the relevance relation are the *truth-grounds* of the atoms in the premisses and conclusion. When we work out the full truth table for, say, $P \supset (Q \supset P)$, we need to know the truth-possibilities of Q just as much as we need to know those of P. They are just as essential and relevant to determining that truth table as are the truth-possibilities of P. It is only in retrospect that we can say we find, in our survey of the completed truth table, that it does not matter if Q is true or false. That is to say, while Q can be any old statement, its *truth-grounds* cannot be any old truth-grounds. That may seem disingenuous, since any old Q always has the same two assignable truth-values in modern classical logic, but it is not. For we cannot write the truth-values in the column for Q in a truth table in any old way, but must provide a systematic mix-and match matrix of all the possible combinations of truth-grounds of all the atomic statements.

How well do the relevantists know the logic diagram tradition or the great modern classical logicians on conclusion containment? The two volumes of *Entailment* range from nothing to almost nothing on Euler, Leibniz, Kant, Bolzano, Venn, Peirce, Frege, Russell, Wittgenstein, or Quine. And how well do recent diagram logicians such as Shin or Greaves know the relevance tradition? They never or almost never mention Anderson and Belnap, Sylvan, or relevance logic, much less see that their own diagrammatic validity is a form, not to say the primary form, of logical relevance. I wanted to bring these two groups together for mutual understanding of what they so deeply have in common.

The ontologists of whole and part are no better. They are concerned with ontological analysis of things, not with logical relevance of inferences. And they have more than enough to do. But they, or someone, should be interested in the consequences of their compositional views for relevant inference.

The thesis that a conclusion necessarily follows if and only if it is in *some* sense contained in the premiss(es) seems to be a basic synthetic a priori intuition many on both sides would accept. The thesis that truth-ground containment is *the* basic sense, or at least *a* basic sense, of relevant containment is a second basic synthetic a priori intuition which I accept, I think many modern classical logicians would accept, and I hope relevantists will at least consider. If I am right that these two theses are basic, then perhaps no positive argument for them should be expected, since that would seem to require more basic premisses. Of course, we may note that these intuitions have been shared enough to be traditional, if not universal. That might permit a special sort of empirical probability argument, if we can avoid the fallacies of appeal to traditional authority or popular belief. Of course, we should look for indirect or dialectical arguments. One would be that relevantists have nothing better to offer than intuition for their views either. Anderson and Belnap basically admit as much, and even make a virtue of having no positive theory. But that is just a tu quoque (ad hominem). Another argument would be that relevantists beg the question if they simply assume that their intuitions are better. But that relevantists beg the question does not prove that they are wrong. And perhaps the second thesis begs the question just as much against the relevantists. A third argument is, what reason is there for thinking truth-ground containment is *not* a form of logical relevance? But that commits the fallacy of appeal to ignorance.

But I think the best argument is a positive one. My theory is actually a synthesis of both sides. It cancels the claim of each side to have the sole truth, reveals each side to be a limited viewpoint, and preserves and transcends the merits of each side in a comprehensive unified theory in which, broadly speaking, one side is the genus and the other side is the chief species. Mere relevantists by definition cannot have such a theory, since it involves admitting modern classical logic is relevant. Nor can mere modern classical logicians, if by definition they cannot admit that relevantist logic is legitimate logic. But my closest antecedents, David Lewis, Restall, Schurz, and Weingartner, give me reason to hope that many logicians may be open to this sort of synthesis, with both sides having an honored and worthy place in relevance logic.

If I myself were arguing against the possibility of relevantist logic, understood as the attempt to formalize extensionally our intensional intuitions about relevance, my argument would be that "there is no backward road from denotations to meanings" (Russell 1905: 487), that is, from extensions to intensions. For the correspondence of extensions to intensions is one-infinitely many. No truth-functional extensional logic can determinately capture the intensional intuitions of any relevantist, since infinitely many other intensions will pick out the same extensions too (Russell 1905: 487). And perhaps that does set an ultimate limit on the relevantist enterprise. But I think this is no reason not to pursue relevantist logic. Within that limit, the best maxim is that there is always more to learn. Perhaps there is an ultimate limit to philosophy as a whole, simply due to our finitude. But that is no reason not to pursue philosophy. Within human limits, the best maxim is that there is always more to learn. Indeed, one could say the same of any field of human learning. But that is no reason not to pursue learning at all.

I have another Russellian criticism as well. Anderson and Belnap prefer intension to extension, but never make clear what they mean by those vague and ambiguous terms. Without more, I can only ascribe to them a vague and possibly even ambiguous notion of "intension." In contrast, Russell and Whitehead clearly distinguish at least four different senses of "intension," and by implication at least four different senses of "extension," in *Principia* (see page 111). Thus it might turn out that Anderson and Belnap's supposedly intensional views are really extensional in some sense or senses. In fact, this is just what happens, and we need nothing like Russell and Whitehead's sophisticated distinction of four senses of "intension" to see it. All we need is the simple sense most philosophers use, namely, that to be intensional is to be non-truth-functional. This may be called the primary sense.

Remember, Anderson and Belnap say their view opposes that of "the extensional community (Anderson 1975: 36), and sails against "the prevailing Extensional Winds" (Anderson 1975: 256). They say variable sharing "concerns...logical consequence, and is semantical in character" (Anderson 1975: 33). They say subscripting "has to do with entailment...as the converse of deducibility, and in this sense is...proof-theoretical" (Anderson 1975: 33; see 186 on syntactics and semantics). But what has any of this got to do with intension in the sense of being non-truth-functional?

What is intensional about Anderson and Belnap's logic, anyway? It is just as truth-functional as modern classical logic is. To use their own words, their test of tautological entailment applies to "any old p and q" just as much as modus ponens and disjunctive syllogism do. It matters not at all to their test what p and q *are*, nor what "p" and "q" *mean*, nor even whether p and q are true or false. The *only* difference between Anderson-Belnap and modern classical logic is *which* patterns of "any old p and q" Anderson and Belnap accept. Perhaps their test is *inspired by* intensional ideas, in some sense of "intensional." But it does not follow in the least that their test *is* intensional, certainly not in the primary sense. To think otherwise is to commit what C. D. Broad calls the genetic fallacy (Broad 1968/ 1925: 11–13). Their test is totally truth-functional, exactly like modern classical logic. And insofar as "intensional" means non-truth-functional, there is nothing intensional about their relevantist logic *by definition*. Thus all their talk of intensionality is just a red herring, at least in the primary sense of "intension." For their tautological entailment is a matter of extensional truth-ground containment, just as validity is in modern classical logic. The only thing their test does is impose their own variable sharing constraint on truth-functional validity.

I agree with Barwise that the study of logic diagrams is in its infancy (Barwise: 1996: viii). So is the study of relevance, and philosophy as a whole may be (Butchvarov 1970: 319). This book has been written toward reunion in logic, or at least toward peaceful co-existence, in a Carnapian spirit of mutual tolerance for logicians' freedom to construct various systems for various purposes, and even to use different senses of "extension" and "intension," not to mention "relevant." The main conclusion is that what modern classical logic and relevantist logics have in common is that with respect to relevance, the former is the genus and the latter are species, if the latter accept no inference the former rejects. I hope this is a point of departure for studies of what else they have in common, that is, of what may be universal in relevance logics. Indeed, a species has the genus as one of its two main parts. Thus, just as a lion *is* feline, relevantism *is* modern classical logic.

The relationship is intimate. A species is a qualified genus. It, or more precisely its difference or qualification, is a way a genus can be presented or filtered, as in "the genus of the species lion." Lions are a specific way felines can be conceived or regarded. In the order of cognition, species are primary and genera secondary; intensions are primary and extensions secondary. We may even say that a species difference *is* a filtering intension, or specific mode of presentation, of the genus. But in the ontological order, what must be logically capable of existing first, in order for something else to have an ontological function or reason for being, is primary. In the ontological order, extensions are primary, since intensions function merely as their modes of presentation; and genera are primary, since species (or more precisely species differences) function as their specific modes of presentation (see my 2007: 78). Thus relevance has no reason for being if there is no validity, because relevance is merely how validity presents itself; and intensional relevance has no reason for being if there is no extensional (truth-ground) relevance. But we are able to cognize the latter in itself, without necessarily viewing it through the filter of the former. More precisely, we can understand truth-ground relevance without understanding any one form of intensional relevance in particular, much as we can understand what it is to be a feline even if we have seen no lions in particular. Indeed, if we are merely interested in valid truth preservation, we can do without intensional relevance at all, just as, if we are merely interested in the higher levels of zoology, we need not concern ourselves with lions at all. At the same time, felines cannot exist unless at least one species of felines exists. Now, by parity of reason, the relevantists are logically guaranteed a place in logic. But this is not on pain of extensional relevance's otherwise being an existing genus which has no existing species. For as shown in the previous chapter, we can admit at least five modern classical constraints on modern classical logic, and by mixing and matching them, many more than five species *within* modern classical logic. Each species of modern classical logic will have some form of extensional relevance as opposed to the intensional relevance of the sort the relevantists say they are concerned with.

This is not to say Plato is right that the more generic a thing is, the more real it is. It is merely to say that a genus logically can exist in reality ("in re") even if a certain one of its species does not. For example, felines can exist even if lions do not, since other felines can exist. And it is to say that just as "the species of the genus feline" logically cannot single out any one species in particular, so "the (species of) intensional relevance of (the genus) extensional relevance" logically cannot single out any one type of intensional relevance in particular. For genus-species relationships are logically capable of being one-many. But "the extensional relevance of validity" logically must single out truth-ground containment in particular, since this is not a genus-species relationship but a necessary one-one correspondence, a synthetic a priori informative identification. For an argument is formally valid if and only if its conclusion is extensionally relevant. Nor is there anything wrong with there being a synthetic a priori truth at the bottom of formal deductive analytic logic. Indeed, it can scarcely be otherwise, on pain of its not being a foundational insight. Or more cautiously, counterexamples do not seem forthcoming to this foundational biconditional. Of course, you may still simply believe the relevantists are right that modern classical logic is wrong.

If I am right that a universal logic would be all about classification, then the deepest sense in which Aristotle is the father of logic is his concept of a classificatory science, which helps us organize our conception of relevance into a science or organized series of classifications. Species differences are the filters or constraints, or going in the other direction, the permissions, releases, or safety valves. Insofar as logic diagrams are the key to such a science of relevance logic, this gives a most general meaning to the metaphor of logical space, which Wittgenstein reserved for his own particular logic. On this scientific concept of relevance, many logicians on both sides of the house have implicitly already been working for decades, if not centuries or millennia. Paradoxically, I would suggest that they ignore classification and simply work out their logical intuitions into the best logics they can, and classify later. Of course, a good classificatory scheme can facilitate, organize, and help direct fruitful exchanges. This is not just a Carnapian spirit of tolerance. Conceiving the inconsistencies of rival logics as series of filters or constraints paradoxically makes these very inconsistencies the basis of a harmonious order, exactly as lions cannot be lambs, but both can live in classificatory peace together as mammals. For the inconsistencies are precisely the differences in definition by genus and difference in relevance science.

This simple, ancient taxonomic approach to universal logic can succeed even if all the more sophisticated recent approaches fail (Béziau 2007/2005 is a good survey). And we can add taxonomic indexing simply by assigning a prefix to the index numbers for each logic we admit as a species. For example, Logic L would have index numbers L1, L2,..Ln. Closures can be prefixed too. If all the premisses and rules of inference used in an L-valid proof are L-theses and L-rules, then the conclusion is an L-thesis. We may also cross-index each statement and rule of inference with multiple prefixes so as to indicate all the logics in which each occurs as a thesis or rule of inference. This can lead to hybrid closures, such as conjunctive or disjunctive closures. For example, if all of proof P's premisses are theses of both logics L and M, and if the sole rule of inference used belongs to L or M, then P's conclusion is a thesis of L or M, and may be assigned disjunctive prefix L-or-M. This would be disjunctive closure. More complex hybrid closures are left to the reader. We may call any thesis of all the logic-species a universal or U-thesis. Of course, there might be no U-thesis. Perhaps there cannot be, given the nature of a possible logic. For a U-thesis could only be a thesis of the last, most specific logic in a single linear chain, namely, the logic with the strongest filters and thus the fewest remaining theses. Only in that way could the thesis be in all the logics in the chain. But there would be no such single chain, since there are indefinitely many chains branching out from modern classical logic. And no rule of inference could be a U-rule, since Wittgenstein's logic (and no doubt infinitely many others) have no rules of inference at all. But our taxonomic logic does not need a U-thesis in order to be a universal logic. To think otherwise is to commit the fallacies of composition and division—not to mention relevance.

Our universal logic is unlike the later Wittgenstein's ordinary language rope of many strands. Our rope is a formal taxonomic logic whose strands are logics. No thesis need belong to every strand, and no strand need occur along the full length of the rope. But there is a formal hierarchy with a place for every logic and every logic in its place. And to show how much or how little the logics have in common, we may use ordered series of indexing prefixes for their species, genera, families, and so on. For example, where S is the species, G the genus, and F the family, theses of Logic L might be prefixed F1-G3-S98. Thus our universal logic is really more like a tree whose trunk is modern classical logic and whose branches extend in many directions. The logic which is universal is the *including* logic, meaning the tree *as a whole*. It includes every logic and every thesis of every logic in a formally organized classificatory manner. It may even trivially include itself, though not as a proper sub-logic. Thus there is a summum genus that runs through the whole tree after all, namely the feature of belonging to the tree.

It might be objected that this is not what is intended by the term "universal logic," since every logic's being included in the same logical schema is not the same thing as every logic's having any logical features in common. My reply is that this may not have been *seen* as a true traditional answer to the question what do all possible logics have in common, but being included in the same logical schema *is* a logical feature in common. For definition by genus and difference belongs to logic, and has belonged to logic for thousands of years. *No* answer, I think, could be *foreseen*, on pain of the question's being uninteresting. If anything more specific can be added to this general answer, that would be wonderful; but in the meantime, we seem to have at least a minimal answer.

Relevantists have been classifying their logics as stronger or weaker than the best known ones, such as E, R, and T, for decades. I see no a priori reason why our modal intuitions should be any easier or harder to organize than our relevance intuitions. But a classificatory science of modal logics would be easier for two historical reasons. First, classification started almost right away with the S1–S5 series of degrees of modal strength. Second, it has been worked on a few decades longer. Similarly for a science of paraconsistent logics, though they are even newer as a serious formal study than relevance logic. Here one may speak of paraconsistent species differences as either filters or constraints on consistency, or permissions or releases on contradiction. (Here a paradox emerges: one might consistently expect a science of paraconsistent logics to be itself paraconsistent; but on my concept, the very inconsistencies among inconsistent logics are the basis for reconciling them.) Similarly for a science of deontic logics, of epistemic logics, and so on. Areas of logic such as these are the prima facie categories or summa genera of the universal science of logic. No doubt various alternative classifications are possible, with the sole exception of truth-ground containment relevance, which is in reality the sole summum genus, insofar as every deductive logic must preserve truth. And the science of logic is itself logic, since definition by genus and difference belongs to logic. In this respect, logic is more like botany than like, say, ethics. Ethics can be classified too, but I mean in contrast to the sense in which valid inference is obligatory. If botany can be a classificatory science, why not logic?

Must even such a universal classificatory science of logic have external formation rules, an external semantics? Following Carnap and Ayer, and rejecting Heijenoort and Hintikka, I have argued elsewhere for the possibility of a universal logic in the sense that its universal quantifiers range over everything including itself and themselves, by using suitable names and descriptions (Dejnožka 2007: 101–4, n.8; 2003: 81–86). Procrustean levels of semantic ascent are no better than theories of types. They may eliminate some paradoxes, but they eliminate infinitely many innocent statements too. Thus they do not even correspond with the innocent, much less explain what it is to be innocent. And though extremely unlikely, it is logically possible that any existing non-metalogic could have developed as part of a natural language and, more broadly, without having to be defined in some already existing metalanguage or metalogic. Nor, by definition, could the first language (or logic) have grown from a prior metalanguage (or metalogic). These games are played!

Of course, regardless of whether it is a metalogic or is simply the logic itself, it should be clear what the logic of our universal classificatory logic would be. For any classificatory science calls out for syllogistic. And syllogistic calls out for Venn diagrams, or more generally, Vennis balls. Thus our universal logic is a diagram logic. Indeed, a classificatory tree is already a tree diagram.

Purely extensional deduction is the limiting case of purely extensional induction. In deduction, the truth-ground containment is total; in induction, it is partial. Thus we have a concept of partial relevance for induction; see the discussion of Wittgenstein's theory of probability in chapter 7. Thus properly speaking, extensional relevance is the category or summum genus of relevance, and modern classical deductive logic, relevantist deductive logic, and inductive logic are its three main domains.

I close with Carnap's famous words:

Let us grant to those who work in any special field of investigation the freedom to use any form of expression which seems useful to them; the work in the field will sooner or later lead to the elimination of those forms which have no useful function. *Let us be cautious in making assertions and critical in examining them, but tolerant in permitting linguistic forms*. (Carnap 1967/1950: 221, Carnap's emphasis)

For us, Carnap's key words are "no useful function." Consider this modus ponens: If a linguistic form is sufficiently used, then it is (probably) relevantly used. Modus ponens and disjunctive syllogism have been used for millennia and belong to the world's most widely used logic. Therefore they are (probably) use-relevant, and more surely so than Anderson-Belnap. Granted, without the "probably," the Carnapian major premise is a non sequitur. Long use does not imply relevant use. Astrology and other idle pseudosciences are counterexamples. But we can diagram and see logical relevance, or containment of the conclusion. This trivializes the major premise to: If we can see that a form is relevantly used, then it is relevantly used. But it also seems the best reason for tolerance of the many kinds of relevance.

Notes

Introduction

1. For a good introduction to Anderson and Belnap, see Anderson (1968: 76–110).

2. The relevantists quibble with some aspects of modern classical tree diagrams as put-up jobs. For example, Jon Michael Dunn calls certain features of Jeffrey's coupled tree method "devices" to "wash through" ex contradictione and the inference of $(q \lor \neg q)$ from any old p (Dunn 1976: 152–53). But I think it is what the diagrams aim to represent that they do not like. That is, they are prejudging what is a put-up job. And if the diagrams successfully show truth-ground containment, then it is too bad if they do not like it.

In general, whether a move is a device or gimmick can depend on one's logical perspective. What is a shabby device from the relevantists' perspective may be essential to ensuring extensional relevance from the modern classical logicians' perspective.

Indeed, the shoe fits the other foot. Meyer calls some relevance logic "cooked" (Meyer 1985: 616 see 621). I would say that insofar as no relevance logic has successfully formalized intensional relevance, *every* relevance logic washes intensional relevance through, either by using some device or by omitting some needed device.

It might be said that this is a mere tu quoque on the part of both sides. But more deeply, Meyer notes that making things come out right in a logic is not necessarily a bad thing. This, too, applies to both sides. But modern classical logic *has* successfully formalized *extensional* relevance. It has succeeded in its aim, while relevance logic has failed so far in its aim. Thus in Meyer's deeper sense, the "put-up job" criticism is actually far more apt for relevance logic. For no matter what devices they use (including entire logics), they are not yet able to make intensional relevance come out right in the first place. Thus, so far, all their devices have been ad hoc, and the proof of that is their collective failure to capture intensional relevance. Of course, this is a matter of degree; surely some relevantist moves are better than others. But there is no backward road from extension to intension.

In an even deeper sense, it is not clear what to count as a device washing through intensional relevance if we do not have a definite picture of what intensional relevance is. We have never seen it clearly, definitely captured at all, washed through or not. This deepens my point about different perspectives. Unlike extensional relevance, we *have* no clear, definite theory of what intensional relevance is. Thus while Dunn's criticism is based on his relevantist perspective, it is based not on a theory of relevance so much as on a more or less well organized family of relevantist intuitions.

Perhaps the deepest question is how natural or artificial formal logic is or should be anyway. Is not everything in a formal logic a formal device in a clear, not to say formal, sense? —And the more formal the device, the better?

3. It is well known that modus ponens and disjunctive syllogism are mutually rewritable.

Anderson and Belnap allow disjunctive syllogism if the "or" is intensional, i.e., non-truth-functional (Anderson 1975: 296–300; see 344; Meyer 1985: 581). For this it suffices that the disjunctive premiss "support corresponding (possibly counterfactual) subjunctive conditionals" (Anderson 1975: 176; see 177). They allow disjunctive syllogism if it is "truth-functional in a *very* special case (as in the theorem of §16.2.3)" (Anderson 1975: 297, their emphasis). They allow that $\Box A$ & $\Box(\neg A \lor B) \rightarrow \Box B$, meaning if there are proofs of the two conjuncts of the antecedent, then there must exist some (possibly quite unrelated) proof of the consequent (Anderson 1975: 299). The "lucky...Meyer-Dunn argument" (Anderson 1975: 299) for this is in (Anderson 1975: §§ 25.2, 25.3).) What they reject is modern classical logic's A & $(\neg A \lor B) \to B$ (Anderson 1975: 299), or any equation of disjunction with genuine implication (Anderson 1975: 255). Restall says, "There are four different proofs of the admissibility of disjunctive syllogism for logics such as E and R.... They all depend on the same first step...the *way up lemma*" (Restall 2006: 311).

Of course, even the modern classical "or" is intensional in some of the modern classical senses of "intension." For Frege, "or" expresses a sense as well as referring to a reference. For a discussion of the senses in which all Fregean senses are intensional, see my (2007: 60–62). Whitehead and Russell distinguish four senses of the word "intension": (1) Propositional functions are intensional if they are not truth-functional, e.g., "*A* believes that *p*" (Whitehead 1978/1910: 8; see 187 for a derivative sense of "intensional proposition"). (2) Propositional functions are intensional if they lack extensional identities—"the same class of objects will have many determining functions" (Whitehead 1978/1910: 23). Such functions are called formally equivalent (Whitehead 1978/1910: 21, 72–73). We may say more generally that different ways of presenting a thing are intensional in this sense. (3) Functions are intensional if their values need not be specified for them to be specified (Whitehead 1978/1910: 39–40). (4) At least by implication, a class is intensional if it is not extensional, where extensional classes ("extensions") are identical if their members are identical (Whitehead 1978/1910: *20.31, *20.43); Whitehead and Russell themselves use only extensional classes. I do not believe Anderson and Belnap ever make it clear which, if any, of these four senses they have in mind, or why they think modern classic logic cannot or does not admit any of them (not to mention Fregean senses), if that is what they think. They merely insist that intensional disjunctive statements "support corresponding (possibly counterfactual) subjunctive conditionals" (Anderson 1975: 176). But I do not see why truth table "or" cannot do just that in infinitely many cases. For each row of a truth table may be said to concern all those possible worlds which make the row have the truth-values it does. And since only one possible world is the actual world, infinitely many counterfactuals would be supported. For example, a disjunctive syllogism involving only *P* and *Q would* be valid regardless of whether any old *R were* true or false; and at least in modern classical logic, *R* cannot be both. I think the all but explicit possible worlds orientation of the *Tractatus* makes this very clear. Also, while by definition truth table "or" cannot be intensional in senses (1) or (4), arguably it is or can be made to be intensional in senses (2) and (3). For example, we can introduce it as primitive and then find it equivalent to some defined version. Thus when we come to the famous "relevantist Dog," who, faced with several roads his master may have taken, concludes that it *would be* and *must be* this road if it *were not* and *could not be* any of the others, I have always had trouble seeing why modern classical disjunctive syllogism would not do perfectly well. Granted, that the Dog cannot smell the master on the other roads is a causal matter. But that merely goes to *evidence* for the truth of the premises of the disjunctive syllogism about which road the master took. We can even set up a disjunctive syllogism about which road has the master's smell, and link it to the main disjunctive syllogism by the material biconditional, "A road has the master's smell if and only if it is a road the master took." Relevantists may dislike putting relevance off to epistemology (compare Sylvan 2000: 47–49 discussing the very different issue of sorites or transitivity); but what is wrong with that for the Dog? Of course, the question what sort or sorts of intensionality "or" has or can have needs more study by both classicists and relevantists. For a brief history of the Dog, see Anderson (1975: 296–300); see also Sylvan (2000: 79–80).

Meyer notes that $((A \supset B) \,\&\, A) \Rightarrow B$ is "a *rule of inference* in Relevant logics and theories" (Meyer 1985: 584), where the double-line arrow stands for metalogical inference or license to infer (Meyer 1985: 585). For modern classical truth-ground containment relevance, $((A \supset B) \,\&\, A) \Rightarrow B$ is true if and only if $((A \supset$

B) & A) → B is, and that is true if and only if $((A \supset B) \& A) \supset B$ is. The rest is filters.

As far as I can see, $((A \supset B) \& A) \supset B$, "$((A \supset B) \& A) \supset B$" is true, and "$((A \supset B) \& A)$" is true $\supset$ "B" is true are all logically equivalent, at least if we take language as changeless. Compare Curt Ducasse's criticism of Carnap that:

> [I]f the process called by Carnap translation from the material into the formal mode of speech is really translation, [then] his conclusion that sentences in the material mode really are disguised syntactical sentences, and therefore that philosophy is really syntax, would not follow. What would follow would be that either they are disguised syntactical sentences, *or* the syntactical sentences into which they are translatable are disguised sentences of the material mode, i.e., are really sentences about objects....
>
> It would thus be perfectly arbitrary which one of such a pair of sentences we chose to describe as a "disguise" of the other, and which one therefore to describe as what the other "really" is; and therefore it would be arbitrary also whether we chose to say that philosophy is really syntax or that syntax, or at least a certain part of syntax, is really philosophy. (Ducasse 1941: 94–95)

Ducasse then criticizes Carnap's claim that this is really translation, since material mode statements are about things and formal mode statements are about words. But for our purposes, the important point is that whether or not they are translations of each other, the corresponding statements are logically equivalent. Compare Tarski's famous "'Snow is white' is true if and only if snow is white." This also appears to kill Quine's criticism that entailment, or some entailment theories, confuse use and mention, since for every use statement there will be a logically equivalent mention statement. We only need to be clear on which is which. See Quine himself on disquotational theory of truth.

Chapter 1

1. Anderson and Belnap (1992: xvii, citing Vojšhvillo 1988) credit Ivan Orlov with starting formal relevance logic; see Restall (2000: 2, citing Došen 1992: 209); Orlov (1928). Anellis provides further cites, which Crayne corrects as: Bazhanov (2007; 2002; 2001; 2001a). See also Bazhanov (2003); Stelzner (2002).

Chapter 2

1. Anthony Edwards shows how to construct Venn diagrams for any finite number of classes by drawing them on topological surfaces of positive curvature, called "Vennis balls" (Edwards 2004: ch. 3), *pace* Venn, who believed his diagrams could be drawn for no more than four classes, since he drew them only on flat planes (Edwards 2004: 9–10). Thus we have three-dimensional visible representation of relevant containment for logical arguments using any finite number of subject and predicate letters.

2. Peirce gives the earliest known truth tables in 1902 (Anellis 2004: 62–63, facsimiles), followed by Wittgenstein and/or Russell in 1912 (Shosky 1997: 20, photocopy of handwriting identified as mainly Wittgenstein's but partly Russell's), and Russell alone in 1914 (Shosky 1997: 23, photocopy of T. S. Eliot's lecture notes). Shosky distinguishes (notational) truth table *devices* from (functional) truth table *technique*, which "is a logically exhaustive analysis of the truth-functions of a given proposition" (Shosky 1997: 13). Shosky finds the latter "evidently familiar" to Whitehead and Russell "as early as 1910, if not before" (Shosky 1997: 18), and used by Frege, Boole, and Philo, if not Aristotle. One might add many Stoics. Shosky and Anellis note we may never know who first used a truth table device.

Landini says Wittgenstein was not the first to publish a truth table, since there is one "[in] Müller's 1909 *Abriss* of Schröder's *Vorlesungen über die Algebra der Logic*" (Landini 2007: 119). See Landini (2007: 120 n.29) citing Müller (1966/1909: 708), and Landini (2007: 120 n.30) citing McGuinness (1988: 162) as well as Shosky (1997) and Anellis (2004). Landini seems unaware that McGuinness (1988) was updated to McGuinness (2005) two years before Landini's (2007) appeared. But it is not important to us here who was the *first* to use truth table technique, use a truth table, publish a truth table or truth table technique, or even see that truth tables explain extensional logical relevance ("following from") as truth-ground containment. What is important to us here is that Wittgenstein *does* see and state this last point, whether he was the first to do so or not; and that Russell *does* endorse the point. And what is more important even than that historical point is the conceptual point that propositional logic *has* a concept of truth-ground containment relevance essentially built right into it.

3. Wittgenstein's theory of propositional contents is just his picture theory of meaning.

4. Black says that Wittgenstein's metaphor of containment is "not notably illuminating" and "is an impediment to clarity. Wittgenstein's main point, however, is that the consequence relation is internal (5.131)" (Black 1970: 240–41). (Of course, "internal" is a metaphor too.) Black has it backwards in the logical order of analysis. For it is the formally clear concept of truth-grounds, as defined by truth tables, that determines and explains the relata of containment as being truth-grounds, and thereby explains the vague metaphor of containment (precisely as containment of truth-grounds), not the other way around. Wittgenstein is simply doing what Anderson and Belnap are trying to do, namely, formalize our vague intuitive notion of containment.

5. Thanks to Charles Pigden for his apt application of Quine's ideology-ontology distinction here.

Chapter 3

1. John Wallis argued in 1631 that the rewrite has an Aristotelian justification (Kneale 1984/1962: 305). Kneale and Kneale find the rewrite "harmless enough" for mere logical inference, as long as we avoid the sort of Leibnizian metaphysics which Russell inveighs against (Kneale 1984/1962: 323).

2. That Bocheński finds this a retrograde step does not detract from its support of my point.

3. Anderson and Belnap cite Kant's subject-contains-predicate theory of analyticity as a precursor of their own theory of entailment (Anderson 1975: 155). And they would agree with me that arguments correspond to hypothetical statements (the conjoined premisses would be the antecedents), which correspond in turn to subject-predicate statements (Anderson 1975: 155).

4. Greaves says, "Frege's...notation...is an example of a blended system which contains elements of both notational styles[, diagrammatic and sentential]" (Greaves 2002: 2; see ch. 10). Greaves says:

> The system of expression which Frege set out in the *Begriffsschrift* seemed to Venn to have a character somewhere between Boolean notation and Venn diagrams. Indeed, Venn wrote that it "deserves to be called diagrammatic almost as much as symbolic." Unlike the diagrams of Euler or Venn, however, Frege's notation does not employ bounded areas as representatives for classes; rather, it uses arcs and lines.... (Greaves 2002: 179; Venn 1971/1894: 493)

Thus "the actual interpretation of his concept-script depends on relationships which are expressed via the geometric relations of lines, arcs, and subformulas" (Greaves 2002: 184–85). Greaves rightly says Frege would not have used diagrams as purely geometrical as Venn's or Peirce's because of Frege's great distrust of intuition in general and of geometrical intuition in particular (Greaves 2002: 183–85). In fact, this is so much so that in Frege's notation, we do not write the conclusion in the very act of writing the premises (except, of course for *A*, therefore *A*). But we might say he *virtually* has visible containment, in that he implicitly has the truth table for modus ponens, and modus ponens is basically his only rule of inference. But the important point is that Frege's formal logic is a truth tree logic. As such, it is no more and no less geometrical than, say, Jeffrey's trees. And it is a diagram logic, since all truth trees are logic diagrams. Basically, it shows truth flow.

Frege does seem to conceive of deduction, or at least of logical equivalence, on a whole-part containment model. One of his chief metaphors is that of carving or splitting up the same propositional content in different ways. The early or pre-sense-reference Frege allows geometrical representation of this, and appears to imply a containment theory of inference. To quote him more fully than I did earlier:

> If we represent the concepts (or their extensions) by figures or areas in a plane, then the concept defined by a simple list of characteristics corresponds to the area common to all the areas representing the defining characteristics; it is enclosed by segments of their boundary lines. With a definition like this, [what we do] is to use the lines already given in a new way for the purpose of demarcating an area. But the more fruitful type of definition is a matter of drawing boundary lines that were not previously given at all. What we shall be able to infer from it, cannot be inspected in advance; here, we are

not simply taking out of the box again what we have just put into it. [But even here t]he truth is that they are contained in the definitions, but as plants are contained in their seeds, not as beams are contained in a house. [Frege's example is as follows:] Often we need several definitions for the proof of some proposition, which consequently is not contained in any one of them alone, yet does follow purely logically from all of them together. (Frege 1974/1884: 100–1)

Frege's example is much like Whately's example of needing to know both premisses of a syllogism to infer the conclusion (see page 131). Frege's presentation is very geometrical. In fact, Frege had already made the point years earlier using Venn-like circular diagrams to represent the logical overlap of extensions of concepts (Frege 1979/1880/81: 33–34). And the later Frege says:

It is possible for one sentence to give no more and no less information than another....If all transformation of the expression were forbidden on the plea that this would alter the content as well, logic would simply be crippled; for the task of logic can hardly be performed without trying to recognize the thought in its manifold guises. Moreover, all definitions would then have to be rejected as false. (Frege 1970/1892b: 46 n.*)

Since the "task of logic" is inference, this appears to imply a containment theory of inference as well. But the important point is that Frege was the first in history to separate syntax from semantics in his writings, implicitly if not expressly, thus implicitly raising issues of soundness and completeness, and making an inference "valid just in case" the truth-conditions of the premises determine the truth-value of the conclusion (Dummett 1981: 81–83). Thus Frege is the origin of modern classical truth-ground containment, at least insofar as such determination can only consist in truth-ground containment.

Bynum says:

> In order to achieve the most accuracy and avoid all error, [Frege] laid down very strict requirements....
>
> (4) The two-dimensionality of the writing surface must be exploited for the sake of perspicuity. The various logical interrelations among the parts of a proposition or a proof must be clearly illustrated in a two-dimensional display, thus making the notation as easy to read as possible.[6]
>
> 6. ...Frege attached no logical or ontological significance to the two-dimensionality of his notation. The two-dimensionality was purely pragmatic: merely a means of achieving maximum perspicuity. (Bynum 1972: 11, 11 n.6)

In contrast, purely linguistic logics are essentially linear, or one-dimensional. Bynum's note 6 is consistent with a logical indifference to linguistic versus diagram logic as such, and playing the ball where it lies. Bynum adds:

> The two-dimensional structure of arrays in Frege's notation makes them very easy to read; for one can tell at a glance how the given propositional expressions are related; and in proofs one can see immediately whether a given derivation conforms to Frege's major rule of inference—a rule of detachment (*modus ponens*). This fits

very nicely with his desire to minimize the possibility of mistakes. (Bynum 1972: 61).

This immediate visibility of a derivation's conformance to the major rule of inference is the next best thing to the visibility of the conclusion in the premisses, and fits very nicely also with Frege's notation as being a halfway house or blend of linguistic and diagrammatic. Bynum says Frege "adopted" the idea from arrays in arithmetic (Bynum 1972: 60). Frege (1977/1879: 5–8) confirms Bynum's account.

5. Anderson and Belnap find it ironic that many modern classical logic textbooks have a chapter on informal relevance fallacies, yet use strict implication or even material implication in their formal chapters, since in their opinion, such relations of implication are not forms of relevant entailment (Anderson 1975: xxi, 17). But as I see it, the real irony is that these formal chapters generally use truth tables and even Venn diagrams to show that to diagram the premisses is already to diagram all valid conclusions. That is, the irony is that these chapters generally *do* show whole-part relevant truth-ground containment, and show it visibly for all to see. Russell's student Copi (1978) and Quine (1959) are stock examples of this. Anderson and Belnap do not seem to know that these things *are* diagrams, much less that they visibly show truth-ground containment. Even more ironically, Anderson and Belnap's gibe applies just as well (or poorly) to their hero, Aristotle. For Aristotle discusses informal relevance fallacies, yet his Barbara syllogism is equatable with hypothetical syllogism. And Aristotle evidently uses literally geometrical diagrams to show the whole-part containment validity of his valid syllogisms, much like Copi and Quine.

6. Carroll calls middle terms "Eliminands" and the other terms "Retinends." He says, "Note that the Eliminands are so called because they are *eliminated*, and do not appear in the Conclusion; and that the Retinends are so called because they are

retained, and *do* appear in the Conclusion" (Carroll 1977/1896: 107, Carroll's emphasis). Compare hypothetical syllogism: $(A \supset B)$ & $(B \supset C)$, therefore $A \supset C$, which some relevantists accept (Gensler 2006: 206; see Weingartner 1994: 102; Diaz 1981: 108).

7. Gardner says,

> Aristotle's way of classifying syllogisms was to divide them into three "figures" depending on the "width" or "extension" of the middle term (i.e. whether it concerned all or part of its class) as compared with the width of the other terms. Later logicians, classifying syllogisms by the *position* of the middle term, added a fourth figure. (Gardner 1968: 32–33, Gardner's emphasis)

Thus it seems Aristotle represents logical extension and position by geometrical extension and position. The great Aristotle scholar W. D. Ross confirms this:

> [M]uch of Aristotle's terminology in [the doctrine of the syllogism] has a mathematical air—["figure," "distance," used of the proposition,] "boundary," used of the term. It is not unlikely that he represented each figure of the syllogism by a different geometrical figure, in which the lines stood for propositions and the points for terms. (Ross 1960: 36–37)

Ross identifies the specific terminological source as theory of proportion (Ross 1960: 37). Ross notes that Aristotle's only model of a developed science was geometry (Ross 1960: 47). Englebretsen says,

We know that Aristotle himself used some kind of diagram system in teaching his syllogistic. This is evident from his vocabulary, if nothing else. He made essential use of (Greek versions of) such terms as "middle," "extreme," "figure," and "term[inus]" (= "end point"). (Englebretsen 1998: 7–8)

Greaves says, "Aristotle himself appears to have employed diagrams, now lost" (Greaves 2002: 116), and cites two "smoking gun" texts from Aristotle in which Aristotle evidently refers to diagrams and to places in diagrams. I shall quote the first text more fully than Greaves does, and I shall also add editor Ackrill's note 3:

> When three terms have the following mutual relation: the last is wholly within the middle, and the middle is either wholly within or not wholly within the first, there must be a perfect syllogism relating the extremes. I call the Middle Term the one that is within another and has another within it; in the lay-out[3] it has the middle place.
>
> 3. Clearly a reference to a diagram, now lost. (*Prior Analytics* 25*b*36ff. as translated and edited in Aristotle 1987: 27; compare Greaves 2002: 116)

I shall quote the second text just as Greaves does, but I shall add editor Ackrill's note 5:

> [W]hat is predicated of both I call the Middle Term; what this is predicated of, the Extremes; the extreme lying nearer the middle, the Major Term; the one lying further from the middle, the Minor Term. The middle is placed outside the terms and first in position.[5]

5. This reference is not to logical relations of terms, but to their places in some diagram. (*Prior Analytic*s 26*b*36ff. as translated and edited in Aristotle 1987: 29; compare Greaves 2002: 116)

Thus it appears that Aristotle himself uses literally geometrical diagrams for his syllogisms—including Barbara, which is in effect hypothetical syllogism. Greaves offers a reconstruction of Aristotle's diagrams for the first three figures (Greaves 2002: 117) and cites Kneale (1984/1962: 71–72) for further discussion.

Chapter 4

1. Russell drew some unpublished maps of the logical form of propositions (Candlish 1996). Russell says, "This question of making a map is not so strange as you might suppose because it is part of the whole theory of symbolism" (Russell 1971/1918: 225). We cannot map the logical form of belief (Russell 1971/1918: 224, 225). But it seems we can map truth-functional conditionals and inferences.

2. I see this as very similar to Kant's two tests of a statement's analyticity: the subject's containing the predicate (relevance), and the statement's denial's implying a contradiction (validity) (Kant 1965/1787: A7–10/B11–18). Surely Kant did not intend his two tests to yield different results. For if their results were not even co-extensive, then they could not possibly both be successful tests of the applicability of the same *concept* of analyticity. As I see it, Kant's first test explains why his second test works. Namely the denial of an analytic (or for us, logical) truth implies a contradiction precisely *because* the subject contains the predicate, so that the predicate is both contained (implicitly affirmed) and denied (see Manser 1968: 197). It merely remains to note that "*P*, therefore *Q*" always corresponds to "If *P*, then *Q*," and to "Statement *P* implies statement *Q*." And this gives us a Kantian argument that valid inference equates to content containment—and specifically, to truth-

ground containment, since *Q* need not expressly occur in *P*. These correspondences logically ground the whole-part containment theory of valid inference in the theory of Locke, Leibniz, and Kant that analytic judgments or tautologous or "trifling" propositions are subject-predicate containments. But in Kantian terms, we must sometimes "think" the predicate in "thinking" the subject very "confusedly" indeed. For the logically basic containment is of extensions or truth-grounds, not intensions or thoughts. But we *can* think them, especially if we have a clear notation to help us.

Anderson and Belnap endorse Kant on analytic containment in statements like "Smith is a bachelor, therefore Smith is unmarried" (note that *Q* does not expressly occur in *P*), and even think Kant would accept addition $(p \rightarrow (p \lor q))$ (Anderson 1975: 155), which they accept (Anderson 1975: 154). But they miss that Kant admits (and even diagrams) disjunctive syllogism, which he presumably thinks would meet his double test of analyticity if rewritten as a conditional statement.

3. A Google book search will find many of these texts. They would take up too much space here.

4. Griffin says, "Russell tries to pick up on [relevant logic's (weaker) variable-sharing condition on entailment] through his notion of formal implication" (Griffin 2001: 293). Russell equates a formal implication with a class of material implications (Russell 1964: 38). If the material implications are not logically true, neither is the formal implication. However, in pure logic, Russell is concerned only with purely general material implications and formal implications, meaning that their only constants are logical constants, that is, logical operators such as "and" or "or." This raises the question whether logical truth is purely general truth, a question which is beyond the scope of this book (see my 2001; 1999: 3, 10–11, 111–12, 116).

Griffin thinks Russell might have anticipated variable sharing relevance as early in 1903, in the first sentence of *Principles*, chapter 1. There Russell says:

> Pure mathematics is the class of all propositions of the form "p implies q," where p and q are propositions containing one or more variables, the same in the two propositions, and neither p nor q contains any constants except logical constants. (Russell 1964: 3)

Call this text #1, and call its requirement "Russell's requirement." In effect, it is a fourfold requirement to: (a) admit only conditional statements (b) of pure logic, (c) pull all the quantifiers to the left (thanks to Torkel Frántzen 2001 for noting this), and (d) ensure that the variable each quantifier governs occur in both the antecedent and the consequent. These may be called Russell's subrequirements (a)–(d). Griffin is evidently asking if this text might anticipate Anderson and Belnap, since theirs is the only type of relevance logic he admits.

Two further texts quickly follow in *Principles* and appear to clarify the first. Text #2 is:

> We assert always in mathematics that if a certain assertion p is true of some entity x, or of any set of entities x, y, z,..., then some other assertion q is true of those entities. We assert a relation between the assertions p and q, which I shall call formal implication. (Russell 1964: 5)

Text #3 is:

> The typical proposition of mathematics is of the form 'F(x, y, z...) implies G(x, y, z...), whatever values x, y, z... may have'...." (Russell 1964: 6)

I have ten comments.

First, Russell's requirement is not a sufficient condition of modern classical validity, so it can scarcely be a sufficient condition of any narrower form of relevant entailment. For example, "$(Fx \lor Gx) \supset (Fx \,\&\, Gx)$" (alternation materially implies conjunction) is not even true, much less logically true. Or more simply, consider "$Fx \supset \neg Fx$" (a statement materially implies its denial). Thus Russell's requirement is a requirement neither of validity nor of relevance (if these can be distinguished), but instead of correct general form for both true and false conditionals.

Second, Russell is concerned in all three texts to characterize pure mathematics, not pure logic. And while Russell aims to reduce mathematics to logic, that would show only that all mathematics is logic, not that all logic is mathematics. In fact, much of logic is not mathematics at all, including the two examples of false statements of pure logic given in the previous paragraph. (Thus these two examples also show that Russell's requirement is too wide.)

Third, all three texts concern quantificational logic. Thus Russell evidently thinks that all mathematics belongs to quantificational logic. In contrast, modus ponens and disjunctive syllogism belong to propositional logic.

Fourth, however, as we saw earlier, statements of propositional logic are always rewritable in quantificational logic. And we can write quantificational versions of modus ponens and disjunctive syllogism which meet Russell's requirement. "$(P \,\&\, (P \supset Q)) \supset Q$" becomes "$(F(x,\ y,\ z...) \,\&\, ((F(x,y,z...) \supset G(x,y,z,...))) \supset G(x,y,z...)$". And "$(P \,\&\, (\neg P \lor Q)) \supset Q$" becomes "$(F(x,\ y,\ z...) \,\&\, (\neg F(x,y,z...) \lor G(x,y,z,...))) \supset G(x,y,z...)$". The rewrites meet Russell's requirement, including subrequirement (d) that all variables x, y, z... occur in both antecedent and consequent. Thus Russell's requirement does not rule out the validity of these forms, much less rule out their having correct logical form for inference. This is the first thing Griffin should have checked, if he really thought Russell's requirement anticipates Anderson and Belnap's variable sharing requirement. Likewise for hypothetical syllogism and other staples of modern classical logic, such as "(P & ¬P) ⊃ Q" and "P ⊃ (Q ⊃ P)", which the reader can easily rewrite.

Fifth, Russell does not indicate whether subrequirement (d) that all variables occur in both antecedent and consequent includes predicate variables as well as individual variables. Must all predicates be quantified over too, so that there will be predicate variables? If so, then all predicate variables would have to occur in both antecedent and consequent as well. And our quantificational rewrites of modus ponens and disjunctive syllogism would then fail to meet subrequirement (d).

But if we take Russell's three texts as logically equivalent, and take texts #2 and #3 as clarifying text #1, then quantification over the predicate letters does *not* seem required. Russell's own example of assertions p and q in texts #1 and #2 seems to make that clear, not to mention his example of predicates F and G in text #3. In fact, in his choice of different letters p and q, and F and G, Russell seems to be insisting on the opposite. Therefore predicate variables do not seem required to occur in both the antecedent and the consequent. Thus our rewrites seem safe.

Sixth, however, even if Russell (or we, acting on our own) *did* extend subrequirement (d) to predicate variables, thus killing our rewrites of modus ponens and disjunctive syllogism, we can still cook up versions of those argument forms which meet subrequirement (d), but which no relevance logician would accept. For example, "(x)(F)(G)((Fx ∨ Gx) & ¬Fx) ⊃ Gx)" fails to include "F" in the consequent. But we can simply add "¬Fx" to the consequent, so that now we have "(x)(F)(G)(((Fx ∨ Gx) & ¬Fx) ⊃ (¬Fx & Gx))." This satisfies subrequirement (d) even if we extend (d) to predicate variables. Yet it is basically just disjunctive syllogism in conditional form, with "¬Fx" innocuously added to the consequent. It is so innocent that "(x)(F)(G)(((Fx ∨ Gx) & ¬Fx) ⊃ ¬Fx)", considered by itself, is merely a version of the rule of simplification, "(A & B) ⊃ B".

Seventh, in traditional whole-part containment terms, Russell's sub-requirement that all variables occurring in the antecedent also occur in the consequent seems puzzling and unnecessary. For relevant containment in arguments means only that the conclusion is contained in the premisses, and not the other way around as well. By parity of reason, we should require only that all variables occurring in the consequent also occur in the antecedent, and not the other way around as well. We should require mutual variable containment only in cases of mutual implication, i.e., logically true biconditional statements. Russell seems to want to ensure that the subject-matter of antecedent and consequent is identical, that antecedent and consequent are about the same entities. But then we need to distinguish identity of subject matter from relevant containment. Perhaps the simplest example distinguishing the two is "(A & B) ⊃ A". The relevant containment of the consequent in the antecedent could scarcely be more obvious, yet it is equally obvious that the consequent does not contain "B". Of course, all mathematical equations equate to logically true biconditionals, but Russell does not limit mathematical statements to equations. All three texts show that he characterizes mathematics in terms of formal implication in general. In fact, all his examples in texts #1–3 are of one-way implications.

Ninth, we have seen that Russell's requirement is consistent with modern classical logic. And what is more, looking to *Principles* as a whole, charity demands that we interpret Russell's requirement to be clearly *intended* by Russell to be consistent with modern classical logic. For there is no doubt that *Principles* is a major work of modern classical logic. Russell accepts modus ponens (Russell 1964: 14), accepts hypothetical syllogism as one of his ten deductive principles (Russell 1964: 16, principle #6), accepts Barbara in two forms (Russell 1964: 31), accepts ex falso quodlibet (Russell 1964: 17), and evidently accepts disjunctive syllogism (Russell 1964: 57–58).

Tenth, I conclude from all this that when Griffin says, "Russell tries to pick up on [relevant logic's (weaker) variable-sharing condition on entailment] through his notion of formal implication" (Griffin 2001: 293), Griffin is ascribing to Russell an intention that is simply not there.

Chapter 5

1. Since Anderson and Belnap take scripts as the necessary and sufficient condition of relevance, and take variable sharing as a necessary condition, it follows from their own view that entailment is in some sense containment that their scripting includes their variable sharing, and a criticism of the latter is a criticism of both.

Chapter 6

1. Greaves cites Barwise (1991) as holding that "'homomorphic' representations [are apparently unable] to naturally represent general negation or disjunction" (Greaves 2002: 183 n.72).

2. Greaves quotes Peirce as saying, "'A *diagram* is a representamen which is *predominately* an icon of relations and is *aided to be so* by conventions. Indices are *also more or less* used'" (Greaves 2002: 172, quoting Peirce 1958/1931–1938: 4.418, my emphasis except for "diagram").

3. In fact we can replace subjunctive conditionals with indicatives using Butchvarov's distinction between objects and entities (Butchvarov 1994: 47), or my distinction between qualified objects and objects in themselves (Dejnožka 2003). On this way out, we must admit some such distinction.

Chapter 7

1. Meyer calls $P \rightarrow (Q \supset P)$ "asserting" the consequent (Meyer 1985: 592, 602), but the traditional fallacy of affirming the consequent is $P \& (Q \supset P)$, therefore Q. In

propositional logic, *P*, therefore $Q \supset P$ ("asserting" the consequent) is a valid argument form, though ruled out by the forward constraint. But the very different $P \mathrel{\&} (Q \supset P)$, therefore *Q* is invalid per se.

Chapter 8

1. "The criticism that the syllogism is question-begging is a traditional one, deriving from antiquity. [See] Cicero's *Academica* (Book II, §§ xiv-xxx) and Sextus Empiricus' *Outlines of Pyrrhonism* (*Outlines*, II, §§ 134–244); *Adversus mathematicos*, II, §§ 300–481" (Gaukroger 1989: 11). Sextus Empiricus gives some specific arguments for this (Gaukroger 1989: 11–15). As part of the early modern revival of skepticism, Descartes (1969/1628: 32, 49), Arnauld (1964/1683: 211–14), and Locke (1959/1690: 401–2) agree that valid syllogisms are circular. Arnauld explains how the "*applicative*" minor premiss specifies or delimits how the "*containing*" major universal premiss implicitly contains the conclusion (Arnauld: 1964/1683: 211–14). Or as Mill puts it:

> In every syllogism the conclusion contains less than is asserted in the two premisses taken together. Suppose the syllogism to be
>
> > All bees are intelligent,
> >
> > All bees are insects, therefore
> >
> > Some insects are intelligent;
>
> one might use the same liberty taken by Mr. Bain, of joining together the two premisses as if they were one—"All bees are insects and intelligent"—and might say that in omitting the middle term *bees* we make no real inference, but merely reproduce part of what had been previously said. Mr. Bain's is really an objection to the syllogism itself, or at all events to the third figure....(Mill 2002/

1891: 110n., Mill's emphasis)

This is intended in terms of class inclusions, but is more deeply a matter of truth-ground containment. Perhaps the best brief discussion is Ross (1960: 41). Woods (2008), who cites Sextus Empiricus (1933: ch. 17) on syllogisms, distinguishes circularity from begging the question, which he analyzes as discursive (compare Aristotle 1962: bk. 2, chs. 5–7, 16). Some say "Aristotle never intended" the syllogism to be "an instrument of discovery," but "a purely expository and didactic device which provided an explanation of a conclusion which was known in advance" (Gaukroger 1989: 31; see 20 citing Barnes 1975: 65–87). This is consistent with the point that if each of two people knows only one premiss, neither can draw the conclusion alone (Whately 1851: 266; see 268–72). That merely shows that each premiss is use-relevant. There is still nothing in the conclusion that is not in the premisses taken together. Also, if this is correct, then Locke's famous critique of the syllogism as useless for discovery is completely misguided, if applied to Aristotle himself.

References

Abeles, Francine F. 1990. "Lewis Carroll's Method of Trees: Its Origin in Studies in Logic." *Modern Logic* 1/1, 25–35.

Allwein, Gerard and Barwise, Jon, eds. 1996. *Logical Reasoning with Diagrams*. New York: Oxford University Press.

Anderson, Alan Ross, Belnap, Jr., Nuel D., and Dunn, J. Michael, eds. 1992. *Entailment: The Logic of Relevance and Necessity*. vol. 2. Princeton, N.J.: Princeton University Press.

Anderson, Alan Ross and Belnap, Nuel D., Jr., eds. 1975. *Entailment: The Logic of Relevance and Necessity*. vol. 1. Princeton, N.J.: Princeton University Press.

———. 1968. "Entailment." In Gary Iseminger, ed., *Logic and Philosophy: Selected Readings*. New York: Appleton-Century-Crofts.

Anellis, Irving. 2009. "Russell and His Sources for Non-Classical Logics." *Logical Universalis* 3/2, 153–218.

———. 2004. "The Genesis of the Truth-Table Device." *Russell* n.s. 24, 55–70.

———. 1990. " A History of Logic Trees." *Modern Logic* 1/1, 22–24.

———. 1990a. "From Semantic Tableaux to Smullyan Trees: A History of the Development of the Falsifiability Tree Method." *Modern Logic* 1/1, 36–69.

Aristotle. 1987. *A New Aristotle Reader*. Ed. by J. L. Ackrill. Princeton, N.J.: Princeton University Press. Quoted by Greaves (2002).

———. 1968. *Physica (Physics)*. Trans. by R. P. Hardie and R. K. Gay. In Richard McKeon, ed., *The Basic Works of Aristotle*. New York: Random House. 1941.

———. 1962. *Prior Analytics*. Trans. by Hugh Tredennick. In *The Categories / On Interpretation / Prior Analytics*. Cambridge, Mass.: Harvard University Press. The Loeb Classical Library.

Arnauld, Antoine. 1964. *The Art of Thinking*. Trans. by James Dickoff and Patricia

James. Indianapolis, Ind.: Bobbs-Merrill. The Library of Living Arts. 5th ed. of 1683 French.

Ashworth, E. Jennifer. 2006. "Medieval Theories of Singular Terms." *Stanford Encyclopedia of Philosophy*. http://www.illc.uva.nl/~seop/entries/singular-terms-medieval/.

Barnes, Jonathan. 1975. "Aristotle's Theory of Demonstration." In Barnes, Malcolm Schofield, and Richard Sorabji, eds., *Articles on Aristotle*. London: Duckworth. Vol. 1: Science.

Bartley, William Warren III. 1972. "Lewis Carroll's Lost Book on Logic." *Scientific American* 227/1, 38–46.

Barwise, Jon. 1996. Preface to Allwein (1996).

———, and Etchemendy, John. 1994. *Hyperproof*. Stanford, Calif.: Center for the Study of Language and Information (CSLI).

———, and Etchemendy, John. 1991. *The Language of First-Order Logic*. Stanford, Calif.: Center for the Study of Language and Information (CSLI).

Bazhanov, Valentin Aleksandrovich. 2007. "Sudba Uchenogo v 'Vek-volkodav'. Evolyutsiya Nauchnykh Vzglyadov I. E. Orlova." In *Istoriya logiki v Rossii i SSSR*. Moscow: Kanon+. In Russian.

——. 2003. "The Scholar and the 'Wolfhound Era': The Fate of Ivan E. Orlov's Ideas in Logic, Philosophy, and Science." *Science in Context* 16/4, 535–50.

———. 2002. "Evolyutsiya Nauchnykh Vzglyadov I. E. Orlova. Sud'ba Uchenogo v Vek-volkodav." In *Ocherki Sotsialnoi Istorii Logiki v Rossi*. Simbirsk-Ulyanovsk: Izdat. Srednevolzhskogo Nauchnogo Tsentra. In Russian.

———. 2001. "Uchenyi i Vek-volkodav. Sud'ba I. E. Orlova v Logike, Filosofii, Nauke." *Voprosy Filosofii* 11, 123–135. In Russian.

———. 2001a. *Uchenyi i Vek-volkodav Sudba I. E. Orlova v Logike, Filosofii, Nauke*. Ulyanovsk: UIGU. In Russian.

Bellucci, Francesco. 2019. Book review of the present book. *Studia Logica* 107, 1–5.

Béziau, Jean-Yves, ed. 2007. *Logica Universalis: Towards a General Theory of Logic*. 2d ed. Basel: Birkhäuser Verlag. 2005.

Black, Max. 1970. *A Companion to Wittgenstein's 'Tractatus'*. Ithaca, N.Y.: Cornell University Press. 1964.

Blackwell, Alan F., ed. 2001. *Thinking with Diagrams*. Dordrecht: Kluwer. Reprinted from *Artificial Intelligence Review* 15/1–2.

Bocheński, Innocentius Marie. 1961. *A History of Formal Logic*. Notre Dame, Ind.: University of Notre Dame Press.

Bolzano, Bernard. 1972. *Theory of Science: Attempt at a Detailed and in the Main Novel Exposition of Logic with Constant Attention to Earlier Authors*. Trans. and ed. by Rolf George. Berkeley: University of California Press. 1837 German.

Brady, Ross. 2003. "Recent Developments I." in Ross Brady, ed., *Relevant Logics and Their Rivals, Vol. 2: A Continuation of the Work of Richard Sylvan, Robert Meyer, Val Plumwood and Ross Brady*. Aldershot, England: Ashgate.

Broad, C. D. 1968. *The Mind and Its Place in Nature*. London: Routledge & Kegan Paul. 1925.

Butchvarov, Panayot. 1994. "The Untruth and the Truth of Skepticism." *Proceedings and Addresses of the American Philosophical Association* 67/4, 41–61. Presidential Address, Central Division.

———. 1970. *The Concept of Knowledge*. Evanston: Northwestern University Press.

Bynum, Terrell Ward. 1972. Prefatory material to Frege, *Gottlob Frege: Conceptual Notation and Related Articles*. Trans. and ed. by Bynum. Oxford: Clarendon Press.

Candlish, Stewart. 1996. "The Unity of the Proposition and Russell's Theories of Judgement." In Ray Monk and Anthony Palmer, eds., *Bertrand Russell and the*

Origins of Analytical Philosophy. Bristol, U.K.: Thoemmes Press.

Carnap, Rudolf. 1967. "Empiricism, Semantics, and Ontology." In *Meaning and Necessity*. Chicago, Ill.: The University of Chicago Press. 1950.

Carroll, Lewis, né Dodgson, Charles Lutwidge. 1977. *Symbolic Logic*. Ed. by William Warren Bartley III. New York: Clarkson N. Potter. Part I, Elementary, 5th ed., 1896. Part 2, Advanced, never previously published. Part 2, Book 7 "The Method of Trees" galley proof mailed November 6, 1896.

———. 1958. *The Game of Logic*. In *Mathematical Recreations of Lewis Carroll: Symbolic Logic and The Game of Logic*. New York: Dover. 1887.

Cheng, Peter C.-H., Lowe, Ric K., and Scaife, Mike. 2001. "Cognitive Science Approaches to Understanding Diagrammatic Representations." In Blackwell (2001).

Clark, Ronald W. 1976. *The Life of Bertrand Russell*. New York: Alfred A. Knopf.

Cooper, W. 1968. "The Propositional Logic of Ordinary Discourse." *Inquiry* 11, p. 297.

Copi, Irving Marmer. 1978. *Introduction to Logic*. 5th ed. New York: Macmillan.

Creighton, James Edwin. 1898. *An Introductory Logic*. 3d ed. New York: Macmillan.

Dejnožka, Jan. 2007. "Dummett's Backward Road to Frege and to Intuitionism." In Randall E. Auxier, ed., *The Philosophy of Michael Dummett*. Chicago and La Salle, Ill.: Open Court. Library of Living Philosophers vol. 31.

———. 2003. *The Ontology of the Analytic Tradition and Its Origins: Realism and Identity in Frege, Russell, Wittgenstein, and Quine*. Reprinted with further corrections. Lanham, Md.: Littlefield Adams.

———. 2003a. "Russell on Modality," *The Bertrand Russell Society Quarterly* 120, 33–38.

———. 2001. "Origin of Russell's Early Theory of Logical Truth as Purely General Truth: Bolzano, Peirce, Frege, Venn, or MacColl?," *Modern Logic* 8/3-4, 21–30.

———. 1999. *Bertrand Russell on Modality and Logical Relevance.* Aldershot, England: Ashgate. Avebury Series in Philosophy.

———. 1981. "Frege on Identity." *International Studies in Philosophy* 13: 31–41.

Descartes, René. 1969. "Rules for the Direction of the Mind." In *The Philosophical Works of Descartes.* vol. 1. Trans. by Elizabeth S. Haldane and G. R. T. Ross. Cambridge, England: Cambridge University Press. 1628 Latin.

Diaz, Manuel Richard. 1981. *Topics in the Logic of Relevance.* München: Philosophia Verlag.

Dorn, Georg and Weingartner, Paul, eds. 1985. *Foundations of Logic and Linguistics: Problems and Their Solutions.* New York: Plenum Press. Selected papers from the Seventh International Congress of Logic, Methodology, and Philosophy of Science, July 11–16, 1983, in Salzburg, Austria.

Došen, Kosta. 1992. "The First Axiomatisation of Relevant Logic." *Journal of Philosophical Logic* 21: 283–336.

Ducasse, Curt John. 1941. *Philosophy as a Science, Its Matter and Its Method.* New York: Oskar-Piest. Republished by Greenwood Press, 1974.

Dummett, Michael. 1981. *Frege: Philosophy of Language.* 2d ed. Cambridge, Mass.: Harvard University Press.

Dunn, Jon Michael. 1976. "Intuitive Semantics for First-Degree Entailments and 'Coupled Trees'." *Philosophical Studies* 29, 149–68.

Edwards, Anthony W. F. 2004. *Cogwheels of the Mind: The Story of Venn Diagrams.* Baltimore, Md.: The Johns Hopkins University Press.

Englebretsen, George. 1998. *Line Diagrams for Logic: Drawing Conclusions.* Lewiston, N.Y.: Edwin Mellen. Problems in Contemporary Philosophy vol. 40.

Ferebee, Ann S. 1975. Review of A. S. Kuzičév, *Diagrammy Vénna: Istoriá I Priménéniá (Venn Diagrams: History and Applications). Journal of Symbolic Logic* 40, 469–70.

Frántzen, Torkel. 2001. Electronic mail to russell-l discussion group.

Frege, Gottlob. 1979. "Boole's Logical Calculus and the Concept-Script." In *Posthumous Writings*, trans. by Peter Long and Roger White, and ed. by Hans Hermes, Friedrich Kambartel, and Friedrich Kaulbach. Chicago, Ill.: The University of Chicago Press. 1880/81 German.

———. 1977. *Begriffsschrift, a formula language, modeled upon that of arithmetic, for pure thought*. Trans. by Stefan Bauer-Mengelberg. In Heijenoort (1967). 1967 English, 1879 German.

———. 1974. *The Foundations of Arithmetic*. 2d rev. ed. Trans. by J. L. Austin. Evanston, Ill.: Northwestern University Press. 1884 German.

———. 1970a. Illustrative Extracts from Frege's Review of Husserl's *Philosophie der Arithmetik*. Trans. by Peter Geach. In (1970c). 1894 German.

———. 1970b. "On Concept and Object." Trans. Peter Geach. In (1970c). 1892 German.

———. 1970c. *Translations from the Philosophical Writings of Gottlob Frege*. Trans. by Peter Geach and Max Black. 2d ed. Oxford: Basil Blackwell. 2d ed. 1960, 1st ed. 1952. Original writings in German.

Gardner, Martin. 1968. *Logic Machines, Diagrams and Boolean Algebra*. Dover ed. New York: Dover. 1958.

Gaukroger, Stephen. 1989. *Cartesian Logic: An Essay on Descartes's Conception of Inference*. Oxford: Oxford University Press.

Geach, Peter. 1980. "Entailment." In 1980b. 1972.

———. 1980a. "Entailment Again." In 1980b. 1972.

———.1980b. *Logic Matters*. Berkeley: University of California Press. 1972.

Gemes, Ken. 2007. "Verisimilitude and Content." *Synthese* 154/2, 293–306.

Gensler, Harry J. 2006. *Historical Dictionary of Logic*. Lanham, Md.: Rowman and Littlefield.

Greaves, Mark. 2002. *The Philosophical Status of Diagrams*. Stanford, Calif.: Center for the Study of Language and Information (CSLI).

Griffin, Nicholas. 2001. Review of my (1999). *Studia Logica* 68/2, 289–94.

Grimm, Robert. 1993. "Individual Concepts and Contingent Truths." In R. S. Woolhouse, ed., *Gottfried Wilhelm Leibniz: Critical Assessments*. vol. 1. New York: Routledge.

Hahn, Lewis Edwin and Schilpp, Paul Arthur, eds. 1986. *The Philosophy of W. V. Quine*. La Salle, Ill.: Open Court. The Library of Living Philosophers, vol. 43.

Hammer, Eric. 1996. "Peircean Graphs for Propositional Logic." In Allwein (1996).

Hawkins, Benjamin. 1997. "Peirce and Russell: The History of a Neglected Controversy." In Nathan Houser, Don D. Roberts, and James Van Evra, eds., *Studies in the Logic of Charles Sanders Peirce*. Indianapolis: Indiana University Press.

van Heijenoort, Jean, ed. 1967. *From Frege to Gödel: A Source Book in Mathematical Logic, 1879–1931*. Cambridge, Mass.: Harvard University Press.

———. 1967a. Introduction to Frege's *Begriffsschrift*. In (1967).

Humphreys, Paul, ed. 1994. *Patrick Suppes: Scientific Philosopher*. Dordrecht: Kluwer. Synthese Library vol. 3, Philosophy of Language and Logic, Learning and Action Theory.

Jeffrey, Richard C. 1967. *Formal Logic: Its Scope and Limits*. New York: McGraw-Hill.

Kant, Immanuel. 1988. *Logic*. Jäsche ed. Trans. by Robert S. Hartman and Wolfgang Schwarz. New York: Dover. 1800 German.

———. 1965. *Critique of Pure Reason*. Unabridged ed. of Kant's 2d ed. Trans. by Norman Kemp Smith. New York: St. Martin's Press. 1787 German.

——. 1950. *Prolegomena to Any Future Metaphysics*. Ed. by Lewis White Beck. Indianapolis, Ind.: Bobbs-Merrill. The Library of Liberal Arts. German 1783.

Kneale, William and Kneale, Martha. 1984. *The Development of Logic*. Oxford: Clarendon Press. 1962.

Kuzičév, A. S. 1968. *Diagrammy Vénna: Istoriá I Priménéniá* (*Venn Diagrams: History and Applications*). Moscow: Izdatéľstvo "Nauka." In Russian.

Landini, Gregory. 2007. *Wittgenstein's Apprenticeship with Russell*. Cambridge, England: Cambridge University Press.

Leblanc, Hugues and Wisdom, William A. 1976. *Deductive Logic*. 2d ed. Boston: Allyn and Bacon.

Lee, Harold N. 1986. "Discourse and Event: The Logician and Reality." In Hahn (1986).

Lewis, David. 1988. "Relevant Implication." *Theoria* 54/3, 161–74.

Locke, John. 1959. *An Essay Concerning Human Understanding*. vol. 2. Coll. by Alexander Campbell Fraser. New York: Dover. Unabridged and unaltered republication of 1st ed. 1690.

Magnani, Lorenzo. 2001. *Philosophy and Geometry: Theoretical and Historical Issues*. Dordrecht: Kluwer.

Manser, Anthony. 1968. "How Did Kant Define 'Analytic'?" *Analysis* 28/6, 197–99.

Mares, Edwin D. 2004. *Relevant Logic: A Philosophical Interpretation*. Cambridge, England: Cambridge University Press.

McDonough, Richard M. 1986. *The Argument of the Tractatus: Its Relevance to Contemporary Theories of Logic, Language, Mind, and Philosophical Truth*. Albany: SUNY Press.

McGuinness, Brian. 2005. *Young Ludwig: Wittgenstein's Life, 1889–1921*. New York: Oxford University Press.

———. 1988. *Wittgenstein: A Life: young Ludwig 1889–1921*. Berkeley: University of California Press.

Meyer, Robert K. 1985. "A Farewell to Entailment." In Dorn (1985).

Mill, John Stuart. 2002. *A System of Logic: Ratiocinative and Inductive, Being a Connected View of the Principles of Evidence and the Methods of Scientific Investigation*. 8th ed. Honolulu: University Press of the Pacific. 1891.

Morris, Thomas V. 1984. *Understanding Identity Statements*. Scots Philosophical Monographs Number Five. Aberdeen, Scotland: Aberdeen University Press.

Müller, Eugen. 1966. *Abriss der Algebra der Logik*. In Ernst Schröder, *Algebra der Logik*. vol. 3. New York: Chelsea Publishing Co. 1909 German.

Orlov / Orloff, Ivan Efimovich. 1928. "The Logic of Compatibility of Propositions." *Matematicheskii Sbornik* 35, 263–86. In Russian.

Peirce, Charles Sanders. 1958. *The Collected Papers of C. S. Peirce*. vols. 1–8. Ed. by Charles Hartshorne, Paul Weiss, and Arthur Burks. Cambridge, Mass: Harvard University Press. 1931–1938.

Popper, Karl. 2007. *Conjectures and Refutations: The Growth of Scientific Knowledge*. London: Routledge. 1963.

———. 1979. *Objective Knowledge: An Evolutionary Approach*. rev. ed. Oxford: Clarendon Press. 1972.

Pietarinen, Ahti-Veikko. 2005. "Compositionality, Relevance, and Peirce's Logic of Existential Graphs." *Axiomathes* 15/4, 513–40.

Quine, Willard Van Orman. 1986. "Autobiography of W. W. Quine." In Hahn (1986).

———. 1986a. "Reply to Harold N. Lee." In Hahn (1986).

———. 1983. *Mathematical Logic*. rev. ed. Cambridge, Mass.: Harvard University Press.

———, and Ullian, J. S. 1978. *The Web of Belief*. 2d ed. New York: Random House.

———. 1976. "Mr. Strawson on Logical Theory." In *The Ways of Paradox*. rev.

and enlarged ed. Cambridge, Mass.: Harvard University Press.

———. 1975. *Word and Object*. Cambridge, Mass.: The M.I.T. Press. 1960.

———. 1959. *Methods of Logic*. rev. ed. New York: Holt, Rinehart and Winston.

Rahman, Shahid. 2001. Review of my (1999). *History and Philosophy of Logic* 22, 99–112.

Read, Stephen. 1988. *Relevant Logic: A Philosophical Examination of Inference*. Oxford: Basil Blackwell.

Restall, Greg. 2006. "Relevant and Substructural Logics." In Dov M. Gabbay and John Woods, eds., *Logic and the Modalities in the Twentieth Century*. Amsterdam: Elsevier North Holland. Handbooks of the History of Logic, vol. 7.

———. *An Introduction to Substructural Logics*. New York: Routledge.

———. 1999. "Negation in Relevant Logics (How I Stopped Worrying and Learned to Love the Routley Star)." In Dov. M. Gabbay and Heinrich Wansing, eds., *What is Negation?* Dordrecht: Kluwer Academic Publishers. Applied Logic Series vol. 13.

Roberts, Don D. 1973. *The Existential Graphs of Charles S. Peirce*. The Hague: Mouton.

Robinson, Richard. 1950. *Definition*. Oxford: Clarendon Press.

Ross, W. D. 1960. *Aristotle: A Complete Exposition of his Works and Thought*. 2d ed. New York: Meridian.

Russell, Bertrand. 1994. *Foundations of Logic 1903–05*. Ed. by Alasdair Urquhart with the assistance of Albert C. Lewis. New York: Routledge. The Collected Papers of Bertrand Russell, vol. 4.

———. 1994a. "Necessity and Possibility." In (1994). Ca. 1903–1905.

———. 1993. *Theory of Knowledge: The 1913 Manuscript*. Ed. by Elizabeth Ramsden Eames in collaboration with Kenneth Blackwell. New York: Routledge. The Collected Papers of Bertrand Russell, vol. 7.

———. 1990. *Philosophical Papers 1896–99*. Ed. by Nicholas Griffin and Albert C. Lewis. New York: Routledge. The Collected Papers of Bertrand Russell, vol. 2.

———. 1987. *Autobiography*. London: Unwin. Vol. 1, 1967.

———. 1985. *My Philosophical Development*. London: Unwin. 1959.

———. 1976. *Human Knowledge: Its Scope and Limits*. New York: Simon and Schuster. 1948.

———. 1974. *An Outline of Philosophy*. New York: Meridian. 1927.

———. 1973. "Is Mathematics Purely Linguistic?" In Russell, *Essays on Analysis*, ed. by Douglas Lackey. London, George Allen & Unwin. 1950.

———. 1971. "The Philosophy of Logical Atomism." In *Logic and Knowledge*, ed. by Robert C. Marsh. New York: Capricorn. 1918.

1969. Introduction to Wittgenstein (1969). 1922.

———. 1968. Letter to Professor C. W. K. Mundle dated December 20, 1968. The Bertrand Russell Archives.

———. 1964, *Principles of Mathematics*. 2d ed. New York: W. W. Norton. 1938.

———. 1960, *Our Knowledge of the External World as a Field for Scientific Method in Philosophy*. 2d ed. New York: Mentor. 2d ed. 1929, 1st ed. 1914.

———. 1954. *The Analysis of Matter*. New York: Dover. 1927.

———. 1919, *Introduction to Mathematical Philosophy*. London: Allen and Unwin.

———. 1905. "On Denoting." *Mind* n.s. 14/4, 479–493.

Schurz, Georg and Weingartner, Paul. 1987. "Verisimilitude Defined by Relevant Consequence Elements. A New Reconstruction of Popper's Idea." In T. Kuipers, ed., *What is Closer-to-the-truth?* Amsterdam: Rodopi. Poznan Studies in the Philosophy of the Sciences and the Humanities, vol. 10.

Sextus Empiricus. 1933. *Outlines of Pyrrhonism*. vol. 1. Trans. by R. G. Bury. London: Loeb Classical Library. Original Greek ca. 200–300 A.D.

Shimojima, Atsushi. 2001. "The Graphic-Linguistic Distinction." In Blackwell (2001).

Shin, Sun-Joo. 2002. *The Iconic Logic of Peirce's Graphs*. Cambridge, Mass.: The M.I.T Press.

———. 1994. *The Logical Status of Diagrams*. Cambridge, England: Cambridge University Press.

Shosky, John. 1997. "Russell's Use of Truth Tables." *Russell* n.s. 17, 11–26.

Stelzner, Werner. 2002. "Compatibility and Relevance: Bolzano and Orlov." *Logic and Logical Philosophy* 10, 137–71.

Stenning, Keith and Lemon, Oliver. 2001. "Aligning Logical and Psychological Perspectives on Diagrammatic Reasoning." In Blackwell (2001).

Suppes, Patrick. 1994. "Comments [on Paul Weingartner (1994)]." In Humphreys (1994).

———. 1957. *Introduction to Logic*. Princeton, N.J.: D. Van Nostrand.

Sylvan, Richard, né Routley, Francis Richard. 2000. *Sociative Logics and their Applications: Essays by the Late Richard Sylvan*. Ed. by Dominic Hyde and Graham Priest. Aldershot, England: Ashgate.

Tarski, Alfred. 1983. *Logic, Science, Metamathematics*. 2d ed. Trans. by J. H. Woodger, ed. by John Corcoran. Indianapolis, Ind.: Hackett. 1st ed. 1956. Original writings in Polish.

Urquhart, Alasdair. 1992. "The Undecidability of all Principal Relevant Logics." § 65 in Anderson (1992).

Varadarajan, Tunku. 2012. "Poisonous Books, Spoilsport Bankers." *Time* 159/15, 7.

Venn, John. 1971. *Symbolic Logic*. 2d ed. Revised and rewritten. Bronx, N.Y.: Chelsea Publishing Company. Textually unaltered reprint of 1894.

Vojšhvillo, E. K. 1988. *Philosophico-Methodological Aspects of Relevance Logic*.

Moscow: Izdatél'stvo Moskovskogo Universiteta. In Russian.

Weingartner, Paul. 1994. "Can There Be Reasons for Putting Limitations on Classical Logic?" In Humphreys (1994).

——— and Schurz, Gerhard. 1986. "Paradoxes Solved by Simple Relevance Criteria." *Logique et Analyse* 113, 29 Année, 3–40.

———. 1985. "A Simple Relevance-Criterion for Natural Language and Its Semantics." In Dorn (1985).

Whately, Richard. 1851. *Elements of Logic*. 9th ed. Boston, Mass.: James Munroe and Company.

White, Richard. 1984. "Peirce's Alpha Graphs: The Completeness of Propositional Logic and the Fast Simplification of Truth Functions." *Transactions of the Charles S. Peirce Society* 20/4, 351–61.

Whitehead, Alfred North and Russell, Bertrand. 1978. *Principia Mathematica*. vol. 1. 2d ed. Cambridge, England: Cambridge University Press. 2d ed. 1927, 1st ed. 1910.

William of Ockham. 1974. *Ockham's Theory of Terms*. Trans. by Michael Loux. Notre Dame, Ind.: University of Notre Dame Press. Part 1 of *Summa Logicae*. Ca. 1323.

Wittgenstein, Ludwig. 1969. *Tractatus Logico-Philosophicus*. Trans. by D. F. Pears and B. F. McGuinness. London: Routledge & Kegan Paul. 1921 German.

Woods, John. 2008. "Begging the Question is Not a Fallacy." In Cedric Dégremont, Laurent Keiff, and Helge Rückert, eds., *Dialogues, Logics and Other Strange Things: Essays in Honour of Shahid Rahman*. London: College Publications.

von Wright, Georg Henrik. 1967. *Logical Studies*. London: Routledge and Kegan Paul. 1957.

———. 1967a. "On The Idea of Logical Truth." In (1967).

———. 1967b. "The Concept of Entailment." In (1967).

Zeman, J. Jay. 1964. *The Graphical Logic of C. S. Peirce*. Chicago, Ill.: University of Chicago: Dissertation.

Index of Names

Index of Subjects

subjunctive conditionals, 35, 61, 110–11, 129; counterfactuals, 110–12

syllogisms / syllogistic, Aristotelian / categorical, 4, 15, 16, 17, 23–24, 26–28, 31, 40–41, 80–81, 96, 97, 107, 118, 120, 121– 23, 130–31

syntax, semantics, and pragmatics, 49

synthetic, 21, 25, 66; a priori, 67, 69, 77, 98–99, 103

T, 106

tautologies, 3, 11, 30–31, 36, 47–49, 54, 63, 84–87, 91, 94–95, 124; see entailment

ticket entailment, 80

truth tables, xiv, xv, 4–5, 13–16, 19–20, 23–25, 29–33, 35, 44, 47, 53, 55, 57, 65, 67–71, 73–74, 76, 79, 87–89, 91, 93, 96–98, 111–12, 114–15, 117, 120

truth trees / tree diagrams, 13–15, 16, 20, 24–25, 27, 29, 31–33, 56, 74, 89, 91, 96, 107, 109, 117; negative / falsifiability, 15, 24, 31, 74; positive, 15, 24

truth-conditions / -makers, 28

truth-grounds, xiii–xiv, 5, 8–10, 13–16, 19, 24–25, 27–28, 30, 32–37,

41–42, 44–49, 54, 55–56, 60, 64–65, 67–72, 73, 76, 78, 84, 87–89, 91, 93–99, 101–3, 107–8, 109, 112, 115, 119, 120, 123–24, 131

truth-likeness (verisimilitude), 37–38

truth-possibilities, 8–9, 14, 28, 44–45, 53, 64–65, 71, 98

truth-values, 9, 13, 15, 28, 38, 47, 65, 70–71, 89, 98, 111–12, 118

use-relevance / relevant use, 34, 40, 79–80, 81, 108, 131

variable sharing, 93; Anderson-Belnap, xiii, 3–5, 7, 25–26, 40, 46–47, 55, 70, 81, 93, 101, 124, 127, 129; Aristotle, 26–28, 40–42; Russell, 124–29

Venn-I, 68

Venn-II, 69

Venn diagrams, see diagrams, Venn

Vennis balls, xv, 20, 24, 107, 114

way up lemma, 111

well-formed diagram (wfd), 22, 68, 80

well-formed formula (wff), 47–48

Made in the USA
Monee, IL
08 June 2020